When Silence Spoke

Where Silence Ends, Cycles Break, and a Daughter's Voice Is Restored

When Silence Spoke

Where Silence Ends, Cycles Break,
and a Daughter's Voice Is Restored

VERONICA MILLS

yo PUBLISHING

When Silence Spoke by Veronica Mills.

ISBN: 979-8-9901758-7-7

Published in the United States by Yosi Publishing, LLC. For more inquiries or permissions, please contact the publisher at www.yosipublishing.com. Cover Design by Daria McFadgen.

This is a nonfiction work. These are the true stories of Veronica Mills. The events and stories in this book are true; however, certain names, identifying details, and locations have been changed to protect the privacy, integrity, and rights of individuals and the author.

To *my beloved daughter:*

You are the reason I chose to heal.
You are the light that led me out of the dark, the laughter that mended my broken places, and the strength that kept me standing when I wanted to give up. You're not just my daughter-you're my best friend, my heart in human form.
This is my story, but it's your legacy.
I love you forever and always.

Contents

Introduction

Have you ever stayed silent—not because you lacked words, but because you feared what might happen if you spoke them out loud? Have you ever learned to survive by becoming smaller, quieter, easier to overlook? For most of my life, silence felt safer than telling the truth.

I learned early how to stay quiet, how to read a room, how to sense when it was better to say nothing at all. Silence became my shield—my way of surviving things I didn't yet have language for and pain I didn't know how to carry. It wasn't that I had nothing to say. It was that I didn't believe my voice would matter if I did.

This book was born from that silence.

When Silence Spoke is not just the story of what happened to me—it's the story of what happened inside me. It is a journey through childhood trauma, addiction, shame, longing, motherhood, faith, and healing, told from the perspective of a woman who spent years pretending she was fine while quietly falling apart. I write this as someone who has lived enough life to know that healing is not linear, tidy, or quick. But it is possible.

What makes this book different is not only the story—it's the structure.

Each chapter shares a piece of my life with honesty and vulnerability. But I do not leave you alone in the telling. After every chapter, you will find two Selah moments—intentional pauses woven into the rhythm of this book. In Scripture, Selah signals a sacred pause, a moment to stop and let truth settle into the soul before moving forward. That is what these are.

This is not a book to rush through.

After each chapter, you will be invited to pause, reflect, and respond. Each Selah includes Scripture, guided reflection, practical action steps, journal prompts, and sacred space for you to write your heart to God. We have intentionally created room in these pages for you to process your own story as mine unfolds.

Because survival shapes belief. And belief shapes identity. If we never stop to examine what we've carried, we will keep carrying it.

Some chapters may feel heavy. Others may feel like relief. Some may awaken memories you thought were long buried. But after every story, there is space—space to breathe, space to pray, space to confront old narratives, and space to invite God into the places that once felt too painful to touch.

I wanted this book to feel like a conversation, not a performance. Like someone sitting beside you saying, You don't have to rush. You don't have to have it all figured out. Let's sit here for a moment. The Selah reflections create room for that—room for your story to surface alongside mine.

Within these pages, you will encounter themes of breaking generational cycles, reclaiming identity, learning to trust God's timing, forgiving yourself, releasing shame, and finding your voice after years of silence. But more than that, you will witness how God gently meets us in the quiet places. How He restores what was hidden. How He heals what was broken. How He calls us out of survival and into freedom.

This is not a book about having all the answers.

It is about telling the truth. It is about acknowledging the ways silence once protected us—and the ways it also kept us stuck. It is about discovering that your voice matters, even if it shakes.

If you have ever felt invisible, unheard, overlooked, or afraid to speak…

If you have learned to survive by shrinking…

If you are tired of carrying what was never yours to hold…

This book is for you.

My story begins where silence once lived. Yours doesn't have to end there.

1

The Mask I Wore

On the outside, I looked like a normal little girl. I smiled when people expected me to. I had reddish-blonde hair that brushed my shoulders, and I always tried to wear my best face—even if I never quite lifted my head. My laughter was forced, and when I said, "I'm fine," what I really meant was, "Help me." I was silently screaming on the inside, but no one seemed to hear. I was seven years old during this season of my life, and already I had learned how to hide behind a smile.

I don't remember the first time I realized I had to hide. It wasn't a conscious decision—more like an instinct. A quiet, invisible shift from child to survivor. I learned early that the world wasn't always safe, especially not at home.

Our home sat on a busy street in a small town—a modest white house with a black roof, the kind that looked cozy from the outside. But looks are deceiving. Inside, the floors creaked beneath worn-out carpet, and the wallpaper peeled at the corners. The scent of cigarette smoke clung to everything—curtains, couch cushions, even my clothes. In the kitchen, the air often carried a sharp mix of stale beer and burnt grease. The TV flickered in the background like white noise, but it couldn't drown out the tension that lived in our walls.

I had both of my parents in the beginning. My dad worked hard and did his best to hold everything together, but the atmosphere in the house was heavy. My mother's drinking was like a shadow that never left—and sometimes, her shadow felt so heavy I stopped breathing. Some days, she was kind and warm, making me giggle with her jokes. But on other days, she disappeared into her bottle, and I'd shrink into her shadow just to go unnoticed. I never knew which version of her I'd get. It was exhausting.

I learned to read her like a book. The way her keys hit the table, the weight of her footsteps, the sound of her sigh told me what kind of night we were going to have. It was like walking through a minefield—every moment tense and uncertain. I became an expert at staying quiet, being helpful, and disappearing when things got bad.

School was my safe haven. The scent of sharpened pencils and floor cleaner, the chatter in the hallways, the gentle hum of classroom routines—it all made me feel grounded. At school, I could exhale. I could laugh without fear of what it would trigger. I could actually be a child. The teachers didn't know what I was going through, but their consistency felt like safety. For those few hours each day, I didn't have to be the emotional sponge, the fixer, or the ghost who moved around the house unnoticed. I got to be me—or at least some version of me.

I wore the mask of "the good girl." The one who didn't cause problems. The one who could handle it. The one who didn't cry or complain. I thought if I was good enough, maybe she would change. Maybe she would choose me over the bottle. Maybe she would see me.

But she didn't.

So I kept wearing the mask. I wore it so long it became second nature—like skin I couldn't shed. It molded itself to my face, to my voice, to the way I carried myself in the world. Over time, I didn't just wear the mask—I became it. The girl who smiled at the right time, who kept everything inside, who showed strength on the outside while quietly unraveling within. I started to believe the mask was who I really was. The strong one. The responsible one. The one who didn't need anything from anyone.

But behind the mask was a scared little girl who just wanted to be held. Seen. Loved.

No one told me that pretending to be okay can become a prison. And no one warned me that the longer you wear a mask, the harder it is to remember your real face.

But I'm learning now. Piece by piece, memory by memory, I'm taking off the mask. Not all at once—some parts still feel safer hidden. But I'm no longer willing to pretend that what happened didn't affect me. I'm not hiding behind "fine" anymore. I want to be free. This is where my story begins.

Before We Continue ...

We need to pause.

In the Psalms, the word *Selah* appears between verses. It isn't rushed past. It isn't explained away. It simply invites the reader to stop. To breathe. To reflect. To let what was just said settle into the soul before continuing.

That is what these Selah moments are.

Throughout this book, after each chapter of my story, you will be invited into one or more Selah reflections. I will not rush you into the next memory, the next wound, or the next layer of healing. Instead, we will pause together. Because survival shapes belief. And belief shapes identity. And if we don't stop long enough to examine what we've carried, we will keep carrying it.

This is not just my story unfolding. It is space for yours to surface, too.

Some chapters will be heavier than others. Some may stir emotions you didn't expect. Some may feel familiar in ways that surprise you. After each one, you will find a Selah — a place to reflect, to pray, to write, to confront old beliefs, and to invite God into places that may have stayed hidden for years.

This first chapter was about a mask.

About the "good girl." About learning to smile when you're silently screaming. About shrinking in order to stay safe.

Maybe you recognized something familiar in those pages. Maybe you didn't grow up in my house, but you learned to read the room just like I did. Maybe you wore a different mask — perfection, humor, independence, silence — but it protected you all the same.

Before we move forward, we're going to sit here for a moment.

The Selah reflections ahead are not interruptions. They are invitations. Invitations to look at your own mask. To examine the beliefs that grew out of survival. To allow God to gently begin uncovering what has been hidden.

You don't have to rush healing. You don't have to have the right words yet. Just pause. Breathe. Let what surfaced in you have space.

Selah.

Selah Moment: Breaking Free from the Victim Mindset

Scripture

In all these things we are more than conquerors through him who loved us. — Romans 8:37 NIV

Reflection

There was a time I believed I would always be the product of my pain. But God has shown me that my identity is not in what I've endured—it's in who He says I am. I am more than what happened to me. And so are you. You are more than the shame. More than the silence. More than a survivor—you are a daughter of the King.

Maybe you've worn a mask too—of strength, silence, perfection, or people-pleasing. Maybe you've smiled while screaming inside. It's time to stop hiding.

As you reflect on where you are, remember this: what you believe about yourself changes everything. When those beliefs align with God's truth, transformation begins. Now it's time to take intentional steps toward freedom. These next actions will guide you in stripping away the masks and living fully in the truth of your identity.

Action

- **Acknowledge the mask.** Identify what you've been using to protect yourself—perfectionism, independence, silence, etc.

- **Bring it to God.** Ask Him to show you how the mask has protected you—and how it's also held you back.

- **Replace the mask with truth.** Speak Romans 8:37 over your life: *"In all these things we are more than conquerors through Him who loved us."* Remind yourself daily who you are in Christ.

- **Take one honest step.** Share your truth with God, yourself, and someone safe. Freedom begins with honesty.

Declaration

I am not what happened to me. I am not the pain I carried. In Christ, I am whole, chosen, and deeply loved. I lay down every mask I've used to survive and choose to walk in truth. I am more than a conqueror through Him who loves me. Today, I walk in freedom, not fear. I am who God says I am—nothing more, nothing less.

Journal

Take a moment to sit with Romans 8:37. Write what it means for you personally to be “more than a conqueror.” How does that truth confront the identity you’ve been living under?

Selah Moment: Embracing Your True Identity

Scripture

Therefore, if anyone is in Christ, the new creation has come: The old has gone, the new is here! – 2 Corinthians 5:17 NIV

Reflection

You are a new creation in Christ. That means your past, your pain, and the labels others gave you no longer define you. When God makes something new, He doesn't just patch it up—He transforms it. The old has gone, and the new has come (2 Corinthians 5:17).

For a long time, I believed lies about who I was—spoken by others and whispered through pain. One teacher once told me I was "too sensitive"—and for years, I wore that label like a warning. I silenced myself to avoid judgment. Another time, someone close to me said I was "hard to love." That lie settled deep in my heart, shaping the way I saw myself in every relationship. But God's Word began to rewrite those beliefs. He calls me chosen. He calls me loved.

Because you are in Christ, you no longer have to live as overlooked, abandoned, unworthy, or broken. Instead, you walk as chosen, seen, redeemed, and whole.

What about you? What lies have you believed? What words have tried to define you? It's time to trade them in for truth.

Action

- **Reflect:** Write down 2–3 lies you've believed about yourself.
- **Replace:** Find scriptures that speak the truth of who you are in Christ (e.g., 2 Corinthians 5:17, Ephesians 2:10, Romans 8:37).
- **Renew:** Speak those scriptures aloud each day. Declare what you're leaving behind—and who you're becoming.
- **Journal:** Write a letter to your "old self," releasing the pain and stepping into the new.

Declaration

Lord, I release the lies I once believed. I am not who others said I was—I am who You say I am. I receive my identity as Your daughter and choose to walk in the new life You've given me. I am no longer bound by shame or old labels. I am a new creation in Christ—whole, loved, and free.

Journal

What words, labels, or messages from your past have shaped the way you see yourself? Sit with them for a moment. Then turn to 2 Corinthians 5:17 and read it slowly. In light of that Scripture, what does it mean for you personally to be a “new creation”?

2

Mom's Bottle, My Burden

There was always a bottle nearby. Sometimes hidden in cabinets, sometimes out in the open like it didn't even matter anymore. But no matter where it was, it always found its way back into her hands.

My mother wasn't just someone who drank—she was someone who disappeared. Her body might've been in the room, but her mind and spirit drifted far away. I used to watch her face change, her speech slur, her warmth evaporate. Some nights she was the life of the party, loud and laughing. Other nights she was a ghost—angry, unpredictable, or completely checked out. And I never knew which version of her I was going to get.

So I learned to watch. To study her. I could tell by the way she moved whether it was going to be a good day or a dangerous one. I became a child with radar—always scanning, always on alert. Never fully relaxed.

I don't think she ever meant to make me carry her pain, but I did. Her addiction wasn't just hers—it wrapped around everything in our home. It shaped how I saw the world. It made me feel like love was something you had to earn, like safety was a luxury, like being a child was something I had to rush through. I grew up fast. Too fast.

And I blamed myself for things I couldn't control.

If I was better, maybe she wouldn't drink so much. If I was quieter, maybe she wouldn't yell. If I helped more, maybe she wouldn't pass out. If I loved her enough, maybe she would stay.

But no matter how hard I tried, the bottle always won. It always took her from me.

There were nights I sat in the dark, listening for her breathing just to make sure she was alive. I cleaned up messes no child should have to touch. I became a peacekeeper, a fixer, a second parent. And I carried it all silently, because there wasn't room for my pain in a house already drowning in hers.

The hardest part wasn't just her drinking—it was the emptiness it left behind. The birthdays she forgot. The promises she broke. The way I started to feel invisible, like I didn't matter enough to make her stop.

Her bottle became my burden. I didn't choose it, but I carried it.

And for a long time, I thought that made me strong. But now I see it for what it really was—survival. A child doing whatever she had to do to get through the day. A daughter loving a mother who wasn't capable of loving her back in the ways she needed.

But that's not the end of the story. Because even though her bottle shaped my beginning, it doesn't define my future. I'm learning now to set it down. To stop carrying what was never mine to hold.

And every time I choose to speak, to heal, to break the silence—I take back something that was stolen.

Selah Moment: Breaking Generational Curses

Scripture

Christ redeemed us from the curse of the law by becoming a curse for us. — Galatians 3:13 NIV

Reflection

Through Christ, we are free from the curses that may have been passed down through generations. Your family's past does not have to determine your future. When Jesus said "It is finished," He broke every chain—addiction, fear, abuse, shame, and cycles of brokenness. What once defined your family line no longer has the right to define you. The old curses lose their grip, and new blessings take root.

Breaking generational chains hasn't been easy for me—but it has been worth it. I am proof that the cycle can end with me. I've seen how patterns of addiction, silence, and shame tried to weave themselves into my story, but through Christ, those chains have been shattered. My daughter doesn't have to inherit my pain. My future is not bound to my family's past.

What about you? Where have you seen the same struggles show up generation after generation? God wants to bring freedom there. He invites you to step into the truth of

Galatians 5:1: "It is for freedom that Christ has set us free. Stand firm, then, and do not let yourselves be burdened again by a yoke of slavery."

Action

- **Identify Patterns:** Write down generational struggles you've noticed in your family (addiction, anger, poverty, silence, fear, shame, etc.).
- **Pray Specifically:** Bring each one to God in prayer. Speak the name of Jesus over them and declare freedom.
- **Replace with Blessing:** For every struggle, write down a scripture that represents God's truth (e.g., instead of addiction → freedom in Christ, instead of shame → Psalm 139:14 worthiness).
- **Declare Daily:** Each morning, declare aloud: "The curse stops with me. God's blessing flows through me."

Declaration

I am a cycle-breaker. In Jesus' name, every chain of generational pain, addiction, or shame is broken. The curse stops with me, and God's blessing begins with me. Freedom flows through my family line now. I walk in the power of Christ, leaving behind the weight of the past and embracing the promise of a redeemed future. Today, I stand firm in my identity as God's child—free, whole, and victorious.

Journal

What unhealthy patterns have you noticed in your family history, and where have they surfaced in your own life? Once you've named them, read Galatians 5:1, 2 Corinthians 5:17, or Romans 8:1. What does it mean that you are not destined to repeat what came before you?

____

____

____

____

____

____

____

____

____

____

____

____

____

____

Selah Moment: Healing from Past Wounds

Scripture

The Spirit of the Sovereign Lord is on me, because the Lord has anointed me to proclaim good news to the poor. He has sent me to bind up the brokenhearted…" — Isaiah 61:1 NIV

Reflection

Jesus did not come only to save souls—He came to heal hearts. The same Spirit that rested on Him to perform miracles and proclaim freedom is the Spirit that meets you in your deepest pain. There is no wound too old, too deep, too hidden, or too shame-filled for His healing touch.

We often try to carry our brokenness alone—tucking it away, numbing it, pretending it doesn't hurt anymore. But unhealed places leak into our relationships, our decisions, our identity, and even our faith. Healing doesn't happen by ignoring pain; it happens when we invite Jesus into it.

There were parts of my story I never wanted to visit again—memories I buried, trauma I avoided, and wounds that felt too tender to touch. I thought silence would protect me. But healing began **in** the silence—when I finally let Jesus into those locked places. He didn't push. He didn't shame me. He gently met me where I was, held what I was carrying, and began to restore what I thought was beyond repair.

Jesus is not afraid of your brokenness. He is not overwhelmed by what broke you. He is not discouraged by how long it has hurt.

Healing is His assignment. Restoration is His specialty. And your broken places are the very spaces He wants to fill with wholeness, comfort, and renewed strength. When the Word says He came to "bind up the brokenhearted," it means His heart moves toward yours with compassion, intention, and power.

You don't have to heal yourself. You only have to bring your heart to the One who can.

Action

- **Name your wounds.** Write down the hurts, memories, or losses that still affect you. Be honest—even if it feels messy or raw.
- **Invite Jesus into each one.** Pray: *"Lord, heal this place in me. Meet me here."*
- **Release what you've been holding.** Surrender anger, shame, fear, or grief—one piece at a time.
- **Replace pain with truth.** Find Scriptures on healing (Isaiah 61, Psalm 147:3, Jeremiah 30:17) and

speak them aloud over yourself.

- **Talk to someone safe.** Healing often deepens when shared with a trusted friend, counselor, or pastor.
- **Pay attention to progress.** Notice small changes—lighter emotions, clearer thoughts, courage to speak, moments of peace. Celebrate them.

Declaration

My brokenness is not a life sentence—it is the door where Jesus meets me. Through His Spirit, healing flows into the deepest parts of my heart. I am not defined by what wounded me; I am defined by the One who restores me. Jesus binds up my broken heart, lifts my burdens, and replaces my pain with His peace, joy, and wholeness. Healing belongs to me, and I walk in that promise today.

Journal

What past wounds still affect my heart, thoughts, or identity? Where do I need Jesus to meet me with healing? What would it feel like to finally lay that wound down and let God replace it with something new?

3

The Day Everything Changed

I was seven.

Old enough to know something felt wrong. Too young to know what to do about it. The room around me glowed with a brightness that made me squint, but inside me, a shadow was forming that no light could touch. It didn't happen at home. I'll leave the details of where to myself. What matters is what it did to me. What it stole. What it silenced.

He wasn't supposed to hurt me. He was someone familiar—someone who should have known better. I had on my favorite pale blue dress trimmed in lace—the most perfect dress, one that felt tainted afterwards. The sound of his voice—calm, casual—clashed with the pounding in my chest. In that moment, everything I understood about safety, trust, and love began to unravel. Outwardly, it was a normal afternoon. Inwardly, my world was splintering like glass.

I didn't have the words for it then. I just remember the sick feeling in my stomach, the way my skin prickled as though warning me. My body froze even as the room hummed with ordinary sounds—the sizzle from the stove, the scrape of a chair on the floor. Something inside me shut down. I left my body in a way only a child in trauma can. I disappeared from myself.

No one noticed.

At home later, the smell of cigarette smoke clung to the curtains while the television droned on in the background. My mother was too far gone in her drinking to see the change in my eyes—the way laughter no longer rose from my chest, the way I flinched at sudden noises. Her bottle, wrapped in a brown paper bag, tilted unsteadily in her hand as her words slurred together. Her half-closed eyes could not meet mine. She didn't ask why I had gone silent. She didn't ask why I suddenly seemed so much older. Maybe she couldn't. Maybe she didn't want to see what was too painful to face. But I was her child. And I needed her to see me.

On the way home, I whispered, "Why? Why? Why?" into the air, my words vanishing like smoke. My small hands clenched into fists in my lap, trying to hold myself together. Inside, I was splintered—like a mirror breaking into a thousand sharp edges. Each shard reflected a different version of me: frightened, silent, unseen. Outwardly, I forced a smile that looked whole. Inwardly, I was nothing but pieces.

I thought maybe it was my fault. Maybe I had done something wrong. I didn't understand how shame could wrap itself around a child who had done nothing to deserve it. I just knew I couldn't talk about it. So I didn't.

I buried it. Deep.

At school, I laughed at jokes, raised my hand in class, and told people I was okay. But every smile was a mask, every laugh hollow. No one could see that inside, I was splintered—a thousand tiny pieces rattling inside me.

That moment—that violation—changed me. It planted a lie deep inside my soul: that I wasn't worth protecting. That I didn't matter. That I wasn't safe anywhere, not even in my own skin.

But here's what I know now: It was not my fault.

Not then. Not ever.

That truth took me years to believe. But speaking it now is one more step toward healing. Every time I tell this part of my story, I take back what was stolen. I reclaim the innocence that was ripped from me. I honor the little girl who didn't have a voice back then—by using mine now.

This is not the chapter that defines me. But it is a chapter I no longer hide.

Selah Moment: Embracing Grace Over Perfection

Scripture

For it is by grace you have been saved, through faith—and this is not from yourselves, it is the gift of God—not by works, so that no one can boast. — Ephesians 2:8-9 NIV

Reflection

You don't have to be perfect to be loved by God. His grace is sufficient in all things. For years I believed I had to earn love—by performing well, achieving more, or never making mistakes. But God met me in my weakness, not in my polished moments. His grace embraced me in the middle of my brokenness and continues to carry me today.

Perfection is a heavy mask we wear, but grace says you are enough as you are. Imagine trying to hold a cracked jar together with your bare hands—exhausting and impossible. That was me. But when I finally released my striving, I found that God's love had been holding me all along. Old labels—failure, not good enough, unworthy—lost their power in the light of His truth. In Christ, I am His daughter, chosen and loved, not for what I do but for who I am in Him.

Action

- **Identify Areas of Striving:** Write down the ways you've been trying to earn love or approval.
- **Invite Grace In:** Pray over those areas and ask God to meet you with His grace.
- **Speak Truth:** Choose one scripture (2 Corinthians 12:9, Ephesians 2:8–9) and declare it over your life daily.
- **Release Control:** Each time you feel pressure to be perfect, pause, breathe, and say, "God, Your grace is enough."
- **Celebrate Progress:** Journal about moments when you felt God's love without earning it.

Declaration

I release perfection and the pressure to perform. I am not defined by my mistakes or achievements. God's grace is sufficient for me. His strength is made perfect in my weakness. I choose rest over striving, trust over control, and freedom over fear. I receive His love today—not because of what I've done, but because of who He is. In Christ, I am enough.

Journal

Where have I been striving for perfection? What would it look like to let God's grace fill that place instead?

Selah Moment: Overcoming Fear

Scripture

For the Spirit God gave us does not make us timid, but gives us power, love and self-discipline. — Timothy 1:7 NIV

Reflection

Fear is not from God. You have been given power, love, and self-discipline to overcome every fear. For years, fear silenced me. It made me shrink back from opportunities, doubt my worth, and stay quiet when I needed to speak. But I've learned that fear does not get to write the ending of my story. Faith does.

Some of us didn't just learn fear — it was forced on us. It was planted in our bodies by someone who should have protected us. That kind of fear doesn't just live in your mind — it lives in your nervous system, in the way you flinch, in the way you scan every room before you sit down, in the way you hold your breath without realizing it. It's the fear of a child who learned that the world wasn't safe, and that the people in it couldn't be trusted.

But God sees the little girl who froze. He sees the woman who still carries that weight. And He says: *that fear is not your identity*. Fear often disguises itself as caution, comparison, or control, but its root is the same — it tells us we are not safe, not capable, not enough. God's Word declares the opposite. In 2 Timothy 1:7 we are promised a spirit not of fear, but of power, love, and a sound mind. That means fear has no authority over your steps — not the fear that was spoken over you, and not the fear that was done to you.

Imagine fear as a shadow on the wall — looming large but powerless once the light is turned on. That's what God's truth does: it exposes fear and shrinks it down to nothing. I've learned to confront fear by naming it and bringing it into God's light. Faith is not the absence of fear — it is choosing to move forward despite it, trusting that God's love surrounds and equips me. And every time I open my mouth to tell my story, I prove that fear lost.

Action

- **Name the Root:** Write down not just what you fear, but where the fear began. When did you first feel unsafe? Bring that memory before God — not to relive it, but to release it.

- **Speak to Your Younger Self:** Write a letter to the little girl who was afraid. Tell her what you wish someone had said: *It was not your fault. You are safe now. You are seen.*

- **Counter With Truth:** Place a scripture where

you'll see it daily — on your mirror, your dashboard, your phone. Let 2 Timothy 1:7, Isaiah 41:10, or Psalm 56:3 become louder than the fear.

- **Pray Boldly:** Ask God to reach into the places fear has hidden — your body, your sleep, your relationships — and replace it with His peace.

- **Take One Brave Step:** Do something today you've been avoiding because of fear, even if it's small. Send the text. Make the call. Say the thing out loud. Courage isn't the absence of shaking — it's moving while you shake.

- **Create a Fear Journal:** Each time fear rises, write it down — and then write God's truth beside it. Over time, you'll see the fear column shrink and the truth column grow.

Declaration

I do not walk in fear. I walk in power, love, and a sound mind. Fear is not my master — Christ is. What was done to me does not define me. The silence that was forced on me has been broken by my own voice. I release every anxious thought, every trauma response, and every lie that told me I wasn't worth protecting. God's perfect love drives out fear — even the fear that was planted in childhood. Today, I step forward in faith, confident that I am equipped, protected, healed, and free. I am no longer the girl who froze. I am the woman who speaks.

Journal

Where has fear been controlling your choices — and can you trace it back to where it started? What would it look like to let God into that earliest memory?

4

Invisible Girl

There's a certain kind of loneliness that lives inside a child who feels unseen. It's not loud or dramatic—it's quiet, heavy, and constant. Like an ache just beneath the surface. It hums under everything, like fluorescent lights in a silent room.

That's what I lived with for most of my childhood. I wasn't just lonely. I was invisible.

My mother was often too consumed by her addiction to notice me. The things most kids could count on—a parent's attention, protection, warmth—I learned to live without. I stopped expecting them. The air at home always smelled faintly of cigarette smoke and something burnt on the stove. Some nights, I'd sit in the hallway listening for her footsteps, hoping this time she'd remember to say goodnight. Other nights, the silence felt heavier than her presence ever did. I learned early that safety wasn't guaranteed, and love wasn't something you could beg for. I started shrinking, disappearing little by little, until I wasn't sure I existed at all unless someone needed something from me.

I became the background in my own life.

I remember trying so hard to be noticed. Not in a loud way, but in small ways: good grades, doing chores without being asked, being quiet and obedient. I thought if I could be enough—good enough, helpful enough, invisible enough—maybe someone would see me and choose me. Maybe my mom would finally put the bottle down and hold me.

But that moment never came.

It's a strange thing to feel like a ghost while you're still alive. To be in a room full of people and feel like you're not really there. I could be smiling, talking, even laughing—and still feel completely unseen. My laughter sounded bright on the outside but felt hollow, like echoes in an empty hallway.

There were nights I'd cry into my pillow, letting the fabric absorb my voice. Not loudly, just enough to let the ache escape. No one came. I began to believe that my feelings were a burden, that needing love was weakness, that being invisible was somehow safer than being disappointed again.

So I stayed small. I stayed quiet. I stayed hidden.

But deep down, there was a part of me that still longed to be found. To be held. To be looked at and not passed over.

That part of me never died. And it's because of her that I'm still here.

Now, years later, I find myself doing something I never thought I'd do: looking into the mirror, holding my own gaze, and whispering, "I see you."

I know now that I was never truly invisible—I was just unseen by people who didn't know how to see me. And their blindness doesn't define my worth.

I see her tears, her courage, her longing. Sometimes, I wrap my arms around myself—just for a moment—and whisper the words she never heard: "You are safe now." It's a small gesture, but one that reminds me to speak kindly to her, to nurture her with tenderness.

You were never too much. You were never not enough. You deserved to be loved. You always mattered.

And now, I'm learning how to live like I believe that's true.

Selah Moment: Trusting in God's Plan for You

Scripture

For I know the plans I have for you," declares the Lord, "plans to prosper you and not to harm you, plans to give you hope and a future. — Jeremiah 29:11 NIV

Reflection

Trust that God's plan for your life is good, even when things don't go as you expect. I remember walking through seasons where I truly wondered if God had forgotten me. Disappointments, delays, and detours made me question everything I believed about His goodness. But over time, I began to see a pattern—God was weaving something beautiful beneath the surface, even when I couldn't see it.

Sometimes, trusting God feels like standing in the middle of a storm with no umbrella, but faith reminds us that He is both the shelter and the One who calms the winds. What I once saw as closed doors or unanswered prayers were actually divine redirections. Looking back, I realize that His plan was never delayed—it was right on time, just not on my timeline.

His faithfulness is steady, even when my faith is shaky. And that's okay. His plan isn't dependent on my perfection—it's built on His promises.

Action

- **Write It Out:** Journal your current dreams, worries, or unanswered questions. Let them spill onto the page.

- **Lay It Down:** Pray and tell God you surrender these things into His hands.

- **Find a Scripture Anchor:** Choose a verse that reminds you of His faithfulness (e.g., Jeremiah 29:11, Proverbs 3:5–6).

- **Declare Daily Trust:** Speak this truth over your life each morning: "God's plan for me is good, and He is working even when I can't see it."

- **Take the Next Step:** Move forward in faith—do one small thing today as an act of trust.

- **Examine Patterns:** What are the things I've been holding onto too tightly? What would it look like to fully surrender them to God today?

Declaration

I trust God's plan for me. It is good, full of hope, and perfectly timed. Even when I don't understand the process, I believe in His promise. I surrender my timeline and embrace His, knowing He sees the whole picture. I am safe in His hands, steady in His grace, and confident that nothing is wasted in His plan for my life.

Journal

What are the things I've been holding onto too tightly? What would it look like to fully surrender them to God today?

___

___

___

___

___

___

___

___

___

___

___

Selah Moment: Understanding Your Worth

Scripture

But you are a chosen people, a royal priesthood, a holy nation, God's special possession, that you may declare the praises of him who called you out of darkness into his wonderful light. — 1 Peter 2:9 NIV

Reflection

You are chosen, valuable, and loved. Your worth is not based on performance or others' opinions but on God's unwavering love for you. For so long, I searched for my worth in places that could never fill me—people's approval, accomplishments, relationships. Each time I came up empty, I believed I had to try harder, do better, be more. But when I finally turned my heart toward God, I realized my worth had never been lost—it was already mine through Christ.

God's love is not conditional; it doesn't shift with your success or failure. He saw you at your lowest and still called you His own. You are His special possession, chosen not because of what you do, but because of who He is. He delights in you. He calls you radiant, royal, and redeemed.

When we begin to truly believe that, we stop chasing love that was never meant to sustain us and start resting in the One who already calls us beloved. We trade striving for surrender. We move from insecurity to identity. The same God who called you out of darkness is still calling you to walk confidently in His wonderful light.

Action

- **Write a Love Letter to Yourself:** Begin with, *"Dear Chosen One…"* Remind yourself of how God sees you—forgiven and loved beyond measure.

- **Anchor in Truth:** Read Ephesians 1:4–5 and Romans 8:38–39. Highlight phrases that remind you of God's unconditional love.

- **Reject the Lies:** Write down the false beliefs you've carried about your worth. Cross them out and replace them with God's truth.

- **Pray for Confidence:** Ask God to help you see yourself through His eyes and walk boldly in your identity as His daughter.

- **Affirm Daily:** Each morning this week, declare, "I am chosen, cherished, and complete in Christ."

- **Act Like You Believe It:** Do something that reflects your worth—set a boundary, celebrate a win, or simply rest without guilt.

Declaration

I am chosen by God, called by name, and loved without condition. My worth does not waver with the opinions of others or my own mistakes—it is anchored in the heart of my Creator. I am His special possession, a reflection of His light and grace. I choose to walk in the confidence of being chosen, to live as one who is deeply loved, and to let my life declare His praises. I am no longer striving for acceptance—I already belong.

Journal

Where have I searched for worth apart from God? What would my daily life look like if I truly believed I am already chosen, loved, and enough?

____

____

____

____

____

____

____

____

____

5

Learning to Pretend

Pretending became my survival skill.

I don't remember when I started, only that one day it just became natural. It was safer to fake a smile than to explain the ache inside. It was easier to say "I'm fine" than to try to find the words for a pain that felt too big—and too messy—to speak out loud.

So I learned to pretend.

I pretended that I wasn't scared when my mom came home drunk.

I pretended I wasn't disappointed when she forgot something important.

I pretended I didn't notice the looks from other adults when they realized what kind of home I came from.

I pretended I was okay when I absolutely wasn't.

At school, I was the "well-behaved" one. Quiet. Polite. A good student. I knew how to *read a room*, how to say what people wanted to hear, how to shrink myself down to avoid attention. I smiled when I needed to. Laughed on cue. Hid the truth so deeply that even I started to believe the version I was performing.

Because the truth felt dangerous.

The truth was that I was hurting. That I felt forgotten. That I felt abandoned. That I hated going home. That I wished I could be someone else—somewhere else. But where could I say that? Who would have listened?

So I kept pretending. I played the role I thought I had to: the strong girl. The independent girl. The girl who didn't need help, didn't cry in front of people, didn't break.

But behind closed doors, the mask would slip.

I cried quietly into my pillow. I talked to God sometimes, not really sure if He was listening. I longed for someone to notice that I was performing my way through life—because maybe then they'd ask what I was really feeling. Maybe then I'd get to stop acting and start healing.

But no one asked. And when no one asks, the pretending gets heavier.

There were moments I wanted to scream the truth: *This is too much. I'm too young to carry this. I'm not okay.* But I didn't. I stayed in character, afraid of what would happen if I let the truth out. Yes, looking back, pretending protected me from falling apart. But it didn't keep me from healing wholly. I had become so good at performing, smiling when I wanted to scream, and showing up when I needed to sit down. I mistook survival for strength. Healing doesn't happen there. It happens in the pause, in the stillness where you stop trying to be fine and start telling the truth. It is messy and tender, but it is where the real work begins. Now, I am unlearning the pretending. I am learning to sit with my pain, to let God touch the places I once hid, and to trust that feeling does not make me weak. It makes me whole.

I'm learning that it's okay to tell the truth, even when it's uncomfortable. I'm learning that being honest about my pain isn't weakness—it's courage. I'm learning that I don't have to wear a mask to be loved. And slowly, gently, I'm letting my real self be seen.

Selah Moment: Letting Go of Jealousy

Scripture

For where you have envy and selfish ambition, there you find disorder and every evil practice. — James 3:16 NIV

Reflection

Jealousy brings disorder into our hearts and robs us of peace. It sneaks in when we compare our lives to others, whispering that we are behind, overlooked, or less valuable. But the truth is, God's blessings are not limited. There is no shortage in His kingdom. Someone else's success does not diminish your worth, and their blessing does not take away from what God has in store for you.

But here's what we don't often talk about: jealousy is its own form of pretending. When you've spent your life learning to mask your pain, to smile when you're breaking, to perform "okay" for the world—envy becomes another layer of that performance. You scroll through someone's life and smile on the outside while something inside you whispers, *Why does she get that and I don't?* You congratulate someone through clenched teeth, then go home and sit in silence with the ache. You pretend their blessing doesn't sting. You pretend you're happy with where you are. But underneath the mask, jealousy is quietly eating away at the peace God wants to give you.

Sometimes jealousy isn't even about wanting what someone else has—it's about grieving what you never got. When you grew up without stability, without being seen, without a mother who was fully present, watching someone else live in wholeness can feel like a personal wound. That's not selfishness—that's unhealed pain wearing a jealous disguise. And until we name it, we'll keep pretending it isn't there.

I've wasted time comparing my life to others, watching their milestones and quietly asking, "Why not me?" It only left me bitter and small. But I've come to realize that their blessings don't take away from mine. There's room for all of us to flourish in God's timing. When I stopped pretending I was fine and got honest about the envy I was carrying, God began to replace it with something real—gratitude that didn't require a mask. When I learned to celebrate others from a genuine place, my heart became lighter, and I grew more confident that God's timing for me is perfect.

Action

- **Identify Comparison Triggers:** Reflect on areas where jealousy often rises—friendships, career, family, or personal milestones. Be honest about where you've been pretending to be okay while quietly envying someone else's life.

- **Name the Real Pain:** Ask yourself—*Am I jealous of what they have, or am I grieving what I never received?* Write down what's underneath the envy. Sometimes jealousy is just unhealed loss wearing a mask.

- **Pray for the Person:** Intentionally bless someone you've compared yourself to. Thank God for their success and ask Him to continue working in their life. This breaks the power of pretending and replaces it with sincerity.

- **Shift the Focus:** Each time you're tempted to compare, write down one way God has already blessed you. Let gratitude dismantle the performance.

- **Celebrate Actively:** Reach out to someone you've felt jealous of. Send a word of encouragement, celebrate their achievement, or simply speak kind words over them — and mean it. Real freedom comes when you no longer have to fake the joy.

Declaration

I release jealousy from my heart and refuse to let comparison steal my joy. I am done pretending to be okay while envy quietly consumes me. I take off that mask today. I choose to be honest about what I feel and bring it to God instead of burying it. I celebrate the blessings of others with a full and genuine heart, knowing their success does not diminish my own. What I didn't receive as a child does not disqualify me from what God has for me now. His timing for me is perfect, His plans for me are good, and my portion is secure in Him. I choose contentment, gratitude, and love—not as a performance, but as my truth. I am free to flourish in my lane while cheering others on in theirs.

Journal

Read James 3:16 and Proverbs 14:30. What consequences of envy stand out to you? Now reflect honestly: where has comparison taken root in your heart—and have you been pretending it hasn't? Is your jealousy really about what someone else has, or is it connected to something you lost or never received?

Selah Moment: Living with Purpose

Scripture

Before I formed you in the womb I knew you, before you were born I set you apart; I appointed you as a prophet to the nations." — Jeremiah 1:5 NIV

Reflection

Before anyone ever spoke a word over you—before family shaped you, before life wounded you, before the world tried to define you—God already knew you. He knew your personality, your voice, your strengths, your tenderness, your calling, and even the parts of your story you would one day wish you could erase. And still, He called you *set apart*.

You are not an accident or an afterthought. God intentionally designed you with purpose woven into your every detail. The dreams inside you, the burdens you carry for certain people, the skills that come naturally to you, the compassion you extend, the creativity you hold, the leadership you step into—none of that is random. It is evidence of a calling that existed long before you took your first breath.

For a long time, I questioned if anything about my life had meaning. I wondered why I had walked through so much pain and whether any of it would ever matter. But with God, nothing is wasted. Not the broken places. Not the tears. Not the seasons that felt like setbacks. Over time, I realized that the parts of my story I once despised became the very places God used to give me wisdom, empathy, strength, and purpose. What once felt like disqualification became the proof of my calling.

God does not overlook your story—He authors it. And every chapter, even the painful ones, equips you to walk in what He created you for. You are set apart, chosen, and intentionally placed in this moment of history to make an impact only you can make. Your purpose is not something you have to chase; it's something you uncover as you walk with the One who created you.

Action

- **Reflect on your passions.** What topics, causes, or activities stir something deep inside you? These often point to purpose.

- **List your natural strengths and learned skills.** Consider what others affirm in you and what you feel energized doing.

- **Identify where pain shaped you.** Ask God how

those experiences might equip you to help others.

- **Pray for clarity.** Ask God to reveal the areas where He has "set you apart," even if they feel small or subtle right now.

- **Take one small step.** Choose one passion or gift and use it this week—serve, encourage, speak, create, or mentor someone.

- **Write down insights.** As God highlights pieces of your purpose, capture them so you can begin to see patterns.

Declaration

I was created with intention and set apart with purpose. God knew me, chose me, and equipped me long before I ever understood my calling. Nothing in my life is wasted—every part of my story carries meaning. My voice matters, my presence matters, and my purpose matters. Today, I walk boldly in who God created me to be, trusting that He will lead me into the fullness of my calling.

Journal

What passions or burdens consistently stir my heart? What strengths, talents, or skills has God placed in me that reflect His purpose for my life?

6

The Shame of My Body

There was a time I didn't feel anything toward my body. It was just…there. A shell I lived in. A thing I didn't think much about. But after the trauma, everything changed.

Suddenly, my body didn't feel like mine. It felt like something that betrayed me, something that got me hurt, something I needed to hide. I didn't have the language for it at the time, but I remember the discomfort—the way I started to cover up more, cross my arms over my chest, avoid mirrors, and dread being seen. I'd feel a prickle crawl across my skin when someone looked too long. My body felt like a warning sign, not a home.

I felt exposed, even when fully clothed. Vulnerable, even when no one was around. The quiet hum of a fluorescent light or the creak of a floorboard could make my heart race. I learned to flinch before danger came, just in case.

As I got older, I became hyper-aware of how others looked at me. Every glance felt threatening. Every comment about my appearance made me question if I was safe. Compliments confused me. Criticism crushed me. I never felt beautiful—only watched, judged, or not enough. My clothes became armor—long sleeves in summer, loose fits to erase the outline of my shape.

And inside, I carried the shame like it was stitched into my skin.

Shame for what had been done to me. Shame for the weight I gained or lost trying to disappear. Shame for simply existing in a body that didn't feel safe.

By the time I was a teenager, that shame turned inward. I started to see myself as fat—even when others told me I wasn't. My body became something I constantly battled. I developed an eating disorder in an attempt to feel control, to erase what I thought made me unlovable. Food became both a punishment and a comfort. Every bite felt like a betrayal; every skipped meal, a strange kind of victory.

There were days I hated my reflection. Not because of how I looked—but because of what I had endured in this body. It became the physical reminder of pain I hadn't asked for. I didn't know how to feel at home in it. I didn't trust it. I didn't want to claim it as mine. I'd stare into the mirror, but it felt like looking at a stranger, a haunted version of who I could have been.

But my healing required that I come back to it.

Little by little, I began to realize that my body wasn't the enemy. It wasn't to blame for what happened. It wasn't dirty or broken or shameful—it was wounded. It had protected me the best it could. It had carried me through every terrifying night, every silent scream, every forced smile. And somehow, it kept me alive.

That's not weakness. That's resilience.

Faith began to help me see through a different lens. Scriptures like Psalm 139 whispered truth into my heart: *"I praise you because I am fearfully and wonderfully made."* It felt impossible at first—but over time, those words became more than verses. They became lifelines.

Now, I'm learning to speak to my body with kindness. I'm learning to look in the mirror and see a survivor, not a stain. I'm learning that my worth isn't in how my body looks, but in the soul it holds. Some days I trace the outlines of my stretch marks and call them survival lines.

The shame is still there sometimes—it whispers, it lingers. But it no longer owns me.

This body, my body, is not something to apologize for. It's not a source of shame.

It's the place where I live. And I'm learning, for the first time, to call it home.

A few days ago, I stood barefoot in the grass, letting the morning sun warm my skin. I took a deep breath, placed my hand over my heart, and whispered, "Thank you." Not because everything is perfect—but because I am still here. And that is sacred.

Selah Moment: Overcoming Body Shaming

Scripture

I praise you because I am fearfully and wonderfully made; your works are wonderful, I know that full well. — Psalm 139:14 NIV

Reflection

Your body is a beautiful creation of God. Let go of any negative self-talk about your body and choose to see yourself as God sees you. For years, I stood in front of mirrors only to find fault. I picked apart every perceived flaw, comparing myself to others and believing my worth depended on how I looked. But slowly, through grace and truth, I've learned that God's reflection of me is far more accurate than my own.

Your body is not a mistake—it is a masterpiece. It holds your strength, your story, your scars, and your survival. Every heartbeat is evidence of divine craftsmanship. When we speak poorly about our bodies, we are criticizing something God Himself called good. Healing begins when we start to see our reflection through His eyes—beloved, beautiful, and purposefully made.

Take a moment to consider this: God designed your hands to create, your legs to carry you forward, your eyes to witness beauty, your voice to bring life. You are His image bearer. You don't have to earn His approval—you already have it.

Action

- **Mirror Moment:** Stand in front of a mirror today and look into your own eyes. Speak truth aloud: "I am fearfully and wonderfully made."
- **Gratitude Practice:** Thank God for three specific things your body allows you to do—walk, breathe, hug, create.
- **Rewrite the Narrative:** Replace each negative thought about your body with a declaration of gratitude or strength.
- **Scripture Meditation:** Read Psalm 139:13–14 and 1 Corinthians 6:19–20. Reflect on what it means that your body is God's temple.
- **Daily Affirmation:** For the next seven days, begin your morning by thanking God for how He created you.

Declaration

I am fearfully and wonderfully made. My body is not a burden—it is a blessing. I honor the Creator by honoring His creation. My body is a temple of strength, beauty, and purpose. I release shame, silence comparison, and choose gratitude. I walk with confidence, knowing I am crafted by the hands of God Himself.

Journal

What negative words have I spoken over my body? What truth from God's Word can replace those lies today?

____

____

____

____

____

____

____

____

____

____

____

____

Selah Moment: Living Free from Shame

Scripture

Therefore, there is now no condemnation for those who are in Christ Jesus. — Romans 8:1 NIV

Reflection

Shame holds you back from experiencing the fullness of God's grace. It whispers lies that you're not enough, that your past defines you, and that healing is for others—not you. But in Christ, those lies are silenced.

I used to carry shame like a second skin—tight, suffocating, and invisible to most. It wrapped itself around memories I never spoke of, decisions I regretted, and wounds I wished no one could see. Shame told me I was unworthy of healing or love. But Jesus met me in the middle of my brokenness—not after I cleaned it up. He saw it all and loved me still.

The Bible says there is no condemnation for those who are in Christ (Romans 8:1). That means no guilt trip, no shame spiral, no labels from your past. Just grace—abundant, undeserved, and freely given. God's grace isn't just about being forgiven—it's about being made whole.

Let today be the day you stop rehearsing your regrets and start receiving your redemption.

Action

- **Name It:** Write down something you feel ashamed of—something you've buried or tried to forget.
- **Surrender It:** Rip up the paper as a symbolic act of surrender. Say aloud, "I give this to You, God."
- **Replace It:** Open your Bible and find one verse that speaks truth to that shame. Meditate on it.
- **Speak Life:** For the next 3 days, speak one truth about your identity in Christ each morning.
- **Forgive Yourself:** Write a letter of grace to your past self. Be as kind as Jesus would be to you.

Declaration

Shame has no hold on me. I am not defined by what I've done or what was done to me. I am fully forgiven, deeply loved, and forever free in Christ. His grace covers my past, His truth shapes my present, and His promises secure my future. I walk boldly—not in guilt—but in the light of God's mercy. I am redeemed. I am whole.

Journal

What shame have I been holding onto that Christ already paid for? What truth does God want me to believe instead?

7

Craving Love in All the Wrong Places

When you grow up without consistent love, you don't stop needing it. You just start looking for it anywhere you think it might show up.

I was desperate to be chosen, to be seen, to feel like I mattered to someone. Anyone. I didn't know what real, healthy love looked like—only that I wanted it so badly I was willing to settle for anything that felt close.

So I started searching.

Sometimes it looked like trying to be "the good girl," hoping that if I was perfect enough, someone would stay. Sometimes it looked like accepting crumbs of attention from people who only wanted parts of me, not all of me. And sometimes it looked like mistaking control, jealousy, or intensity for love—because no one had ever taught me the difference.

I told myself lies like:

"If I give more, they'll love me back."

"If I change who I am, maybe I'll finally be enough."

"If I let them take what they want, maybe they'll stay."

But they didn't stay. And I was left emptier every time.

I confused validation for love. Affection for intimacy. Attention for worth. And I let people into my life who mirrored the dysfunction I was raised in, because it felt familiar—even when it hurt.

It's hard to admit that sometimes I chose people who mistreated me, not because I didn't know better, but because I believed that was the best I could get. I had been taught, without words, that love was something you earned by shrinking, pleasing, or giving yourself away.

And even when I knew it wasn't real love, I clung to it. Because loneliness felt worse.

But none of it filled the hole. None of it healed the ache. Because what I really needed couldn't be found in the arms of someone else—it had to be rebuilt inside of me.

I needed to love *me.*

To see myself as worthy apart from who wanted me.
To stop chasing love from those who were only ever meant to be lessons.
To recognize that real love doesn't confuse, control, or cost you your self-worth.

Healing has meant learning to be alone without feeling abandoned.
It's meant learning to say "no" to what feels familiar but unsafe.

It's meant waiting for the kind of love that doesn't require me to disappear in order to be held.

I still crave love. That hasn't changed. But now, I crave the *right* kind—the kind that sees me, respects me, honors me, and adds to who I already am.

And every time I choose myself over the wrong kind of love, I prove to that little girl inside me that she is worth more than being used, ignored, or replaced.

She is worthy of a love that stays. And so am I.

Selah Moment: Trusting God with Your Future

Scripture

Trust in the Lord with all your heart and lean not on your own understanding; in all your ways submit to him, and he will make your paths straight. — Proverbs 3:5-6 NIV

Reflection

Trusting God with your future means loosening your grip on the need to control every detail and learning to rest in the truth that He is already ahead of you—preparing, guiding, and making a way.

There was a season when I believed I had to map out every step of my life—plan it perfectly, control the outcomes, avoid mistakes. But life doesn't follow our blueprints. Detours came. Delays discouraged me. I often asked, "God, where are You in this?" And yet, every time I look back, I see His hand was never absent. It was in the closed doors that redirected me. It was in the silence that grew my faith. It was in the waiting where trust took root.

And for some of us, the hardest thing to trust God with isn't a career or a calling—it's our hearts. When you've spent years chasing love from people who could never give it to you the way you needed, surrendering your desire to be chosen feels terrifying. But trusting God with your future means trusting Him with who He brings into it—and who He removes. The love you've been craving doesn't start with someone else. It starts with trusting that God's love is enough to fill what others never could.

Surrender isn't giving up—it's giving *over*. It's laying our unknowns at His feet and saying, "Lead me, Lord—even when I don't see the road." His Word says He makes our paths straight (Proverbs 3:5–6), not always visible, but always purposeful.

You may not know what's next, but you can know who holds your next. And He is faithful.

Action

- **Name the Fear:** Write down one area of your life where you're struggling to trust God (e.g., relationships, finances, calling).
- **Surrender Your Heart:** If you've been holding onto a relationship, a pattern, or a version of love that costs you your peace, write it down and release it to God. Tell Him: *I trust You with my heart, even the parts that are afraid to be alone.*
- **Visual Surrender:** Place that note in your Bible or prayer journal with the words: *God, I trust You with this.*

- **Seek His Word:** Find 2–3 scriptures about God's guidance (like Jeremiah 29:11 or Isaiah 30:21) and post them somewhere visible.

- **Take the Next Step:** Do one small thing today that shows trust—make the call, pray the prayer, take the leap.

- **Pray Boldly:** Ask God to give you peace that surpasses understanding as you follow Him, even when the path is unclear.

Declaration

I release the need to control what I cannot see. I trust that God is working behind the scenes on my behalf. His plans for me are good, His timing is perfect, and His ways are higher than mine. I walk forward with faith, not fear. I will not be overwhelmed by uncertainty—I will be anchored in His promises. I will no longer search for love in places that leave me empty. I trust God to bring the right people into my life and to heal the places where the wrong ones left damage. My worth is not determined by who stays or who leaves—it is sealed by a God who chose me before I ever had to perform for it. God is leading me, step by step, and I choose to follow. My future is safe in His hands.

Journal

What's one part of your future that's been hard to surrender to God? Have you been trusting people with your heart that God never assigned to your life? How can you practice trusting Him more with both your future and your need to be loved this week?

Selah Moment: Learning to Forgive Yourself

Scripture:

Be kind and compassionate to one another, forgiving each other, just as in Christ God forgave you. — Ephesians 4:32 NIV

Reflection

Sometimes the hardest person to forgive is the one staring back in the mirror. We replay our failures, regret the things we can't undo, and allow shame to take up residence in our hearts—long after God has already let it go.

I've found that forgiving others came easier than extending that same mercy to myself. I could believe God forgave me, but I struggled to believe I deserved to walk in that freedom. Especially when it came to the choices I made chasing love. I carried so much shame for the people I let in, the pieces of myself I gave away, and the times I stayed when I knew I should have walked away. I replayed every moment I settled for less than I deserved and punished myself for being desperate enough to accept it. But desperation wasn't a character flaw—it was a wound. And wounded people don't need more punishment. They need grace.

Guilt became a heavy cloak I wore for years—one that told me I needed to keep punishing myself to prove I was sorry. But guilt is not a tool of God's love. And shame is not a requirement for redemption.

Holding onto guilt keeps us stuck in the past. It makes us believe that we're still bound by the very things Jesus died to set us free from. Grace is a gift—freely given, not earned. And when we refuse to forgive ourselves, we're not just dishonoring our healing—we're also questioning the completeness of God's forgiveness.

There came a day when I realized my self-punishment wasn't making me holy. It was making me bitter, afraid, and spiritually exhausted. That day, I chose to write myself a letter—not of blame, but of grace. I apologized to myself. I forgave myself. I declared that I was no longer going to carry what Jesus had already lifted off me.

I'm still learning, but now I catch myself when the old voice of shame creeps in. I pause. I breathe. And I remind myself: *I am forgiven. I don't have to keep punishing myself for what God already paid for.*

You deserve to walk in that freedom too.

Action

- **Forgive the Person Who Searched:** Specifically release yourself from guilt over past relationships, situationships, or moments where you accepted less than God's best for you. Write down what you've been punishing yourself for and say out loud: *I forgive myself for looking for love in places that hurt me. I was doing the best I could with what I had.*

- **Ask God** in prayer to help you receive His grace fully and to silence the voice of shame.

- **Place a reminder** somewhere visible (a sticky note, a lock screen, a verse card) that says: *I am forgiven. I am free.*

- **Speak out loud each day this week**: "I forgive myself. I will no longer live in guilt."

Declaration

I release myself from the prison of guilt and shame. I choose to walk in the freedom Christ died to give me. I forgive myself—completely, deeply, and daily. I will no longer relive what God has already redeemed. I forgive myself for every time I gave my heart to the wrong person, for every time I confused attention for love, and for every time I stayed too long hoping someone would change. Those choices do not make me foolish—they make me human. And God's grace covers every single one. I am covered by grace, healed by mercy, and free to live without chains. My past does not define me—God's love does.

Journal

What have I been holding against myself that God already forgave? How can you treat yourself with the same compassion you offer to others—especially regarding the choices you made when you were just trying to be loved?

8

When Rejection Feels Like Proof

Some wounds don't bleed. They echo. Rejection was one of the earliest echoes I learned to live with—not always through words, but through absence, through silence, through the quiet ways people left or never showed up in the first place.

As a little girl, I felt the sting long before I could name it. I remember sitting on the edge of my bed, tying my shoes slowly, waiting for someone to notice I was struggling. My mother walked past me, her mind somewhere far away, and my small voice stayed tucked in my throat. The rejection wasn't loud—it was a quiet ache settling beneath my ribs. I'd whisper to myself, *Why am I not enough to stay?*

As an adult, the scenes changed but the emotions didn't. I remember watching someone I cared for lose interest in real time—their texts grew shorter, their tone colder, their presence fading like a light dimming in a room. My chest tightened the same way it did when I was a child, a sinking feeling whispering, *You're easy to walk away from.*

I didn't understand it then, but every time someone overlooked me, forgot me, abandoned me, or chose someone else over me, I made it mean something about me:

I wasn't lovable.

I wasn't enough.

I wasn't wanted.

That's the cruelty of rejection in childhood—you don't see it as someone else's limitation. You see it as confirmation of your own unworthiness.

So I started living like I had to earn my place in people's lives. I tried harder. I people-pleased. I made myself small and easy to love, hoping it would convince them to stay. But no matter how perfectly I behaved or how gently I tried to exist, the rejection still came—sometimes fast, sometimes slow, but always familiar.

The emotional weight was suffocating. Rejection didn't just hurt emotionally—it affected my whole body. My stomach would clench, my breath would shallow, my shoulders would fold inward as if preparing for impact. My mind repeated the same loop: *What did I do wrong? Why am I never enough?*

I internalized lies that shaped everything:

If they leave, it's my fault.

If they ignore me, I must not matter.

If they choose someone else, it proves I'm forgettable.

And those lies showed up everywhere—in relationships where I over-gave, in friendships where I stayed quiet to avoid conflict, in choices where I settled for less because I believed less was all I deserved.

But God began healing me in the most unexpected ways.

The turning point wasn't dramatic. It was gentle—like a truth rising slowly after years of being buried. I remember crying one night, asking God why people kept leaving. And in the stillness, I felt Him whisper to my spirit:

Their rejection is not a reflection of your worth. It is My protection over your life.

That truth didn't erase the pain, but it reframed it.

Looking back, I can see it now: every "no," every closed door, every person who walked away was God guarding me from what would have broken me further. Their leaving wasn't the end of me—it was the beginning of Him rebuilding me.

I had to grieve the losses. I had to sit with the younger version of myself who still panicked at the thought of not being chosen. I had to stop trying to understand why people left—and start reminding that little girl inside me:

You were never the problem. You were never too much. You were never unworthy.

Rejection still stings sometimes. But it no longer writes my story. Now, when someone walks away, I don't crumble. I don't chase. I don't twist myself into knots trying to be enough. Instead, I remind myself: *What's meant for me will never require me to beg, shrink, or prove my worth.*

I am not disposable. I am not invisible. I am not too much or not enough. I am worthy of a love that sees me, stays with me, and celebrates me. And healing began the moment I decided to believe that.

Selah Moment: Focusing on Your Own Growth

Scripture

But one thing I do: Forgetting what is behind and straining toward what is ahead, I press on toward the goal to win the prize for which God has called me heavenward in Christ Jesus. — Philippians 3:13-14 NIV

Reflection

Growth isn't always loud. Sometimes it's slow, quiet, and almost invisible—until one day you look back and realize God has been doing more in you than you ever noticed.

For years, I carried the weight of what I wasn't—who I hadn't become yet, the mistakes I made, the seasons I felt stuck, the moments I wished I could redo. I compared myself to where I thought I *should* be and punished myself for not being there yet. And every rejection I experienced made me believe I was falling further behind—like being left or overlooked was proof that I wasn't growing fast enough, wasn't good enough yet. But rejection was never a measure of my progress. It was just redirection. But God keeps teaching me this: **you can't move forward while staring backward.**

Forgetting what's behind doesn't mean pretending it never happened. It means refusing to let your past failures, regrets, or delays dictate your identity or your direction. It means releasing the version of yourself you've outgrown. It means celebrating that God is not finished with you.

Growth is not a straight line. It's holy progress—one brave step at a time. Some days that step is big. Other days, it's simply choosing not to give up. Both matter. Both count. Both are celebrated by Heaven.

There is beauty in the becoming. There is purpose in the stretching. And there is strength in the pressing. God is shaping you, maturing you, and leading you exactly where you need to be.

Honor the journey. Honor your pace. Honor the God who walks every step with you.

Action

- **Write down three small victories** God has helped you accomplish this month.

- Identify **one area** where you've seen growth—even if it feels tiny.

- **Reframe a Rejection:** Think of one rejection that still stings. Write down how God may have used it to redirect your growth rather than define your worth.

- **Pray:** "Lord, help me release what holds me back and step boldly into what You have for me."
- **Practice grace:** Speak one kind truth to yourself anytime self-criticism rises.
- **Choose a physical reminder** (a journal, a verse card, a note on your mirror) that says: *I am moving forward.*

Declaration

I am growing every day, even in ways I cannot see. I release the weight of my past and step boldly toward the future God has prepared for me. The people who walked away did not take my purpose with them. Every rejection was redirection, and I refuse to let being left behind convince me that I've stopped growing. I press forward with grace for myself, strength for the journey, and confidence in the One who leads me. My progress is real. My growth is holy. My future is secure in Christ.

Journal

What do I need to release so I can move forward? Has a rejection made you feel stuck or behind in life? What signs of growth can you celebrate today—even ones that came out of being turned away?

Selah Moment: Fear of Rejection

Scripture

Accept one another, then, just as Christ accepted you, in order to bring praise to God. — Romans 15:7 NIV

Reflection

You have already been accepted by Christ. People may reject you, but God's love for you is unchanging. I've felt the sting of rejection and carried the weight of not being enough. But God's acceptance has taught me that I am already loved, chosen, and worthy—not because of what I do, but because of who I belong to.

Rejection once felt like a wall that kept me out, but now I see it as a redirection toward deeper truth. God has never turned His face from me. In His eyes, I've always had a place—no striving, no pretending, just grace.

We all long to belong, to be seen and known. But earthly acceptance is fragile. God's love, on the other hand, is unshakable. When people walk away, God leans in. When I feel overlooked, He whispers, "I see you."

Action

- **Remember the Pain:** Reflect on a specific moment of rejection that still hurts.
- **Invite Healing:** In prayer, ask God to touch that wound with His love.
- **Affirm His Truth:** Write down three affirmations from Scripture about who you are in Christ (e.g., Ephesians 1:4–6, Romans 8:38–39).
- **Bless the Space:** Speak a blessing over the place where rejection tried to plant bitterness.
- **Reaffirm Your Identity:** Each morning this week, remind yourself aloud: "I am accepted by God."

Declaration

I am fully accepted in Christ. Rejection no longer gets the final say—God's love does. I am not forgotten, overlooked, or unworthy. I am seen, chosen, and secure. Even when others walk away, my place in God's heart is unshakable. I stand firm in my identity as His beloved.

Journal

Where have I let rejection shape how I see myself? What would change if I truly believed I am fully accepted in Christ?

9

The Memory That Stays

Not all wounds come from harm. Some come from heartbreak.

My father wasn't abusive. He wasn't cruel. He didn't scream or hit or neglect me out of selfishness. In many ways, he was everything a father should be—hardworking, kind, supportive, and steady. When he was around, I felt safe. I felt seen.

He was my hero.

When I was eight, my father left my mother. It was a painful shift, and although I didn't fully understand it at the time, I know now it was not an act of abandonment—it was a choice for peace. He walked away from the chaos, not because he stopped loving us, but because staying would have destroyed something in him. I stayed behind at first, not because he didn't want me, but because I didn't want to leave my mother. I didn't want her to feel abandoned.

But she couldn't care for me. And eventually, the roles reversed—I packed my things and went to live with him.

And that's when I began to see the full weight he carried. He worked long hours and still made time to show up for me. He provided what he could, protected what mattered, and poured love in ways that only a good man can. His love wasn't always loud, but it was consistent. He didn't make promises he couldn't keep. He kept showing up—and that mattered more than anything else.

Still, as a child, I struggled with the emotional tug-of-war. I had so many questions I didn't know how to ask:

Why did he leave?

Was it my fault?

Did he miss me like I missed him?

Even when I moved in with him, a part of me still grieved what we lost when the family split. I missed the sound of his voice in the hallway. I missed the way his laughter filled the house. And yet, I was living with him—under the same roof, wrapped in his love—and I was still learning to reconcile what had changed.

There were moments when his exhaustion spoke louder than his words, and I'd wonder if I was a burden. But deep down, I knew better. I knew his silence was never indifference—it was survival. He was doing the best he could with what he had.

The older I got, the more I understood. He left because he had to. He loved me the best way he knew how. He was fighting his own battles while still trying to be everything I needed.

And that's what makes him a hero in my eyes—not because he was perfect, but because he was present. He was human. And he still chose to carry me forward when things fell apart.

I no longer view that time through the lens of abandonment. I see it through the lens of sacrifice.

He walked away from one kind of chaos so I could have a different kind of peace. He taught me what strength looks like in silence. What love looks like in consistency. What fatherhood looks like when it costs something.

This chapter isn't about blame. It's about honor.

I honor his memory, not just for what he did—but for who he was. A hard-working man who showed up. A protector who made hard choices. A father whose love made an imprint deep enough to stay, even after he was gone.

And I am who I am because of him. Because even in the brokenness, he was my safe place. Even in the distance, he never stopped being my dad.

And even now—I carry him with me.

Selah Moment: Embracing Your Role in God's Kingdom

Scripture:

Now you are the body of Christ, and each one of you is a part of it. — 1 Corinthians 12:27 NIV

Reflection

You were created on purpose, with purpose. You're not an afterthought in the kingdom of God—you're a necessary part of His design.

For a long time, I believed my story made me "less than." I thought my past disqualified me and my wounds made me unusable. I looked at others and saw people who seemed more gifted, more whole, more "qualified" to serve God.

But God doesn't call the perfect—He calls the willing.

Slowly, He began to show me that the very things I thought made me unfit were actually the things that made me effective. My story didn't count me out; it brought depth to my calling. My pain didn't silence me; it gave power to my testimony. My healing didn't just restore me—it equipped me.

Sometimes the people who shaped us most aren't here to see what we've become. But the love they poured into us — even imperfectly — becomes part of the purpose we carry. Honoring their legacy is one of the most powerful ways we step into our role in God's kingdom.

You have a place in the body of Christ that no one else can fill. No one else has your story, your heart, your way of seeing the world. No one carries your exact combination of gifts, compassion, wisdom, and lived experience.

You matter. Your presence matters. Your voice matters.

And the kingdom is incomplete without the part *you* bring.

Action

- **Pray:** "Lord, show me the gifts You've placed inside me."
- **Honor a Legacy:** Write down one way someone's love, sacrifice, or presence shaped who you are today. Ask God how He wants you to carry that forward as part of your purpose.
- Identify **one place** you can serve this week—at church, in your community, or through encouragement to someone who needs it.
- **Take one bold step forward**, even if it's small. Send

the message. Volunteer. Say yes.

- **Ask God** to open doors aligned with your purpose.

Declaration

I am a vital part of the body of Christ. I am chosen, equipped, and anointed for purpose. My story has power, my gifts are needed, and my presence makes a difference. The love that was sown into me — even through imperfect people — was not wasted. It is part of my purpose, and I carry it forward with honor. I will show up boldly, serve faithfully, and walk confidently in the calling God has placed on my life.

Journal

Where is God inviting me to step into purpose? How has someone's love or sacrifice shaped the role you play today? What gifts do I need to acknowledge and embrace? What fears do I need to release so I can serve fully?

____

____

____

____

____

____

Selah Moment: Shifting from Fear to Faith

Scripture

Now faith is confidence in what we hope for and assurance about what we do not see. — Hebrews 11:1 NIV

Reflection

Faith is not built in the moments when everything is clear, predictable, or guaranteed. Faith grows in the dark—when you can't see the outcome, when the future feels uncertain, and when fear tries to fill in the blanks with worst-case scenarios. Fear thrives on the "what ifs," those quiet but persistent whispers that question God's goodness and your security in Him.

But faith speaks a different language. Faith says, *"Even if I don't see it yet, I know God is working."*
Faith says, *"Even if I don't understand, I trust His character."*
Faith says, *"Even if it doesn't happen the way I imagined, God is still good."*

I've had seasons when my mind was flooded with "what if" thoughts—What if I fail? What if I'm not enough? What if things don't work out? But God has been teaching me to shift my perspective. Instead of letting fear dictate my thoughts, I'm learning to anchor myself in "even if" faith. It's the kind of faith that refuses to let fear have the final say.

Faith isn't pretending everything is perfect. It's choosing to believe that God is present, active, and trustworthy in the middle of uncertainty. It's leaning into His promises more than your fears. It's standing on what you know about God rather than what you don't know about tomorrow.

Sometimes the shift from fear to faith means trusting that the people God placed in your life — even the ones you've lost — were part of His plan. It takes faith to believe that love wasn't wasted, that sacrifice had purpose, and that what felt like loss was actually God writing a chapter you couldn't read yet.

When you can't see the path ahead, faith reminds you that God sees perfectly. When your heart feels anxious, faith reminds you that God is steady. When your mind gets overwhelmed, faith reminds you that you are held by a God who never fails.

Action

- **Identify your biggest "what if" fear.** Name it clearly so you can confront it with truth rather than avoid it.

- **Find a Scripture that speaks directly to that fear.** (Examples: Isaiah 41:10, Psalm 56:3, Joshua 1:9, 2

Timothy 1:7.)

- **Trust the Story:** Write down one loss or change that once felt like the end. Now write what God built from it. Let that become evidence for your faith the next time fear rises.

- **Declare truth aloud daily.** Speak your Scripture or affirmation every time anxious thoughts rise.

- **Replace "what if" with "even if."** When fear comes, pause and say: *"Even if ____, God is still faithful."*

- **Take one step of obedience.** Do something small today that demonstrates trust—send the email, make the call, rest, forgive, or move forward despite uncertainty.

Declaration

I refuse to let fear speak louder than my faith. God is in control, even when I cannot see the outcome. I choose courage over worry and trust over uncertainty. I trust that every person God placed in my life — and every one He called home — was part of a story He is still writing. My loss is not the end. It is proof that God's plan is bigger than what I can see. Even if I don't understand what comes next, I know God is good, and He is guiding my steps with purpose and love. My hope is anchored in Him, and I walk forward in confidence.

Journal

What "what if" fear has been dominating my thoughts lately? Has a loss or separation made it harder to trust God's plan? What truth from Scripture can you hold onto when grief tries to disguise itself as fear?

____

____

____

____

____

____

____

____

____

____

____

____

____

____

____

____

10

Performing for Approval

When love feels conditional, performance becomes survival. I didn't learn this from words—it was shaped in me by the way rooms changed depending on how I behaved.

I remember the soft click of my bedroom door as I eased it shut, holding my breath so I wouldn't disturb anyone. The hallway always smelled faintly of Pine-Sol and cigarette smoke, and I'd tiptoe across the creaking boards like a dancer memorizing her marks. If I moved quietly enough, no one got upset. If I smiled at the right time, no one asked questions. If I kept myself small, no one noticed the ache I carried.

From a young age, I learned to measure my worth by other people's reactions.

If I was helpful, I earned a nod of approval.

If I stayed quiet, the tension in the house softened.

If I laughed at jokes that weren't funny, if I swallowed the truth when it burned my throat—that meant I was being "good."

So I became what people needed me to be. The *good girl.* The responsible one.
The quiet one who didn't take up too much room.
The one who folded her feelings into neat squares and tucked them away like clothes that didn't fit anymore.

At school, I scanned faces the way other kids scanned homework instructions—looking for clues, searching for the version of me that would be safe. I watched girls link arms in the hallway and wondered what it felt like to be chosen without having to earn it. Even in church, where people talked about unconditional love, I sat straight-backed in the pew, hands folded, pretending I didn't feel invisible.

I didn't realize it then, but piece by piece, I was disappearing.

The real me—the one with loud questions and quiet hurts, the one who sometimes wanted to slam a door instead of smoothing everything over—she slipped further into the background each time I smiled through something that broke me a little.

And the strangest part?
The applause never lasted anyway.

Approval based on performance evaporates quickly. One wrong move, one off day, one moment of honesty—and suddenly you're not so "good" anymore. So you learn to start over. Tighten up. Try harder. You learn to read the room before you even exhale.

I lived in that cycle for years—earning, pleasing, perfecting—terrified that if I ever stopped performing, someone would finally see the tangled, hurting parts of me…and walk away.

The Turning Point

But life has a way of exposing what we try to hide.

For me, it happened on an ordinary Tuesday. I was sitting in my car in the grocery store parking lot, hands still wrapped around the steering wheel even though the engine was off. I had spent the entire day holding myself together—smiling when I wanted to cry, nodding when I wanted to scream, showing up while feeling hollow.

And something inside me simply…gave out.

My chest tightened, my vision blurred, and before I could swallow it down like I always did, tears spilled onto my lap. Not quiet, polite tears—*ugly, gut-deep sobs* that soaked through my shirt and fogged up the windshield.

For the first time in my life, I couldn't perform. I was too tired. Too stretched. Too empty.

I remember gripping the steering wheel and whispering, "I can't do this anymore."

And right there in that small, metal cocoon—with the smell of stale fast-food wrappers and the radio humming static—I felt something shift.

I wasn't afraid of being seen anymore.

I was afraid of losing myself.

And that fear finally outweighed the fear of disappointing anyone else.

That moment didn't fix everything. But it cracked something open. It made room for truth.

What I Know Now

I was never created to perform for love. I was created to receive it—freely, honestly, fully.

Real love doesn't demand silence. It doesn't reward pretending. It doesn't need you to dress your wounds before showing them.

Real love sits beside you on a hard day and doesn't ask you to smile. It holds space when your voice shakes. It sees you—not the rehearsed version, not the polished version—*you.*

Performing kept me alive long enough to survive my childhood, but that constant act turned into exhaustion I carried into adulthood like a second skin.

Now, I'm unlearning the show. I'm learning to rest instead of hustle. To tell the truth instead of saying "I'm fine." To take up space without apologizing. To let silence be honest instead of heavy.

Some people have drifted away since I stopped performing. That loss stings in places I didn't know still existed. But the people who stayed—the ones who love the unmasked, unedited, unfiltered me—they are proof that real love doesn't need a script.

And perhaps the greatest revelation of all:

I'm learning to give myself the approval I spent decades chasing.

I don't have to shrink to be lovable.

I don't have to earn my right to exist.

I don't have to pretend I'm worthy.

I already am.

Selah Moment: Celebrating Your Strengths

Scripture

We have different gifts, according to the grace given to each of us. — Romans 12:6 NIV

Reflection

God didn't create you as a copy of anyone else. He intentionally wove strengths, desires, talents, and even quirks into you—on purpose and for purpose. The world tries to convince us to fit a mold, to measure ourselves against someone else's abilities, appearance, platform, or calling. But comparison blinds us to the beauty of our own design.

I spent years shrinking myself, believing that what I carried wasn't enough—or worse, that it was somehow wrong. And when you've spent your life performing for approval, celebrating your own strengths feels foreign—almost dangerous. You learned to highlight what others wanted to see, not what was actually inside you. But the gifts God gave you were never meant to be performed. They were meant to be lived in. I'd look at others and assume their abilities were more valuable than mine. But the more I walk with God, the more I realize that what He placed inside me is not accidental. My voice, my sensitivity, my strength, my creativity, my story—they all carry a grace that's perfectly aligned with what He's called me to do.

When I stopped trying to be who others were and started embracing who God made me, I felt freedom. I felt permission. And I felt purpose start to rise. God doesn't want you to hide your gifts out of fear, insecurity, or comparison. He wants you to use them—boldly, joyfully, and with confidence that He placed them in you for a reason.

Action

- **Write down at least five gifts, strengths, or qualities God placed in you.** (Don't overthink it—write what's real, not what you think is "good enough.")

- **Separate Your Gifts from Your Performance:** Write down one strength you know is real — not because someone applauded it, but because it's who you are even when no one is watching. That's the gift.

- **Ask God to show you one gift** you've been minimizing, hiding, or overlooking.

- **Choose one practical way to use one of your gifts this week**—encourage someone, serve, create, speak up, help, share, or support.

- **Speak gratitude out loud** for the way God uniquely designed you.
- **Release comparison.** If there's someone you often compare yourself to, pray over your heart and ask God to help you celebrate them without diminishing yourself.

Declaration

I am fearfully designed and purposefully gifted. God's grace is alive in every strength He placed inside me. I refuse to compare, shrink, or hide. My strengths are not a performance. They don't require applause to be valid. I no longer need anyone's approval to celebrate what God already placed inside me. I boldly embrace the gifts God has entrusted to me, and I will use them to honor Him and bless others.

Journal

What gifts have I overlooked or undervalued in myself? Have you been confusing performance with purpose—doing things for approval instead of from identity? How can you use your God-given gifts with boldness this week—not to earn love, but because they're already yours?

Selah Moment: Breaking Chains of Comparison

Scripture

"We do not dare to classify or compare ourselves with some who commend themselves. When they measure themselves by themselves and compare themselves with themselves, they are not wise." — 2 Corinthians 10:12 NIV

Reflection

Comparison can be a quiet thief, robbing you of joy, confidence, and contentment. I know this struggle well. I've measured my worth by how others looked, what they achieved, or how far ahead they seemed. Social media only made it worse—highlight reels became yardsticks I could never measure up to. And when you've spent your life performing for approval, comparison becomes the scoreboard. You're not just admiring someone else's life—you're measuring whether your performance was good enough to earn what they have. That's not inspiration. That's a chain.

But over time, God began to whisper truth over the lies I had swallowed. He reminded me that I am not called to run someone else's race. My journey is sacred. My pace is intentional. My identity is not found in comparison, but in Christ.

You are God's masterpiece—uniquely created, deeply loved, and fully equipped for your own purpose. There is no one else with your exact calling, experiences, or voice. The world needs your light—not a copy of someone else's.

Let today be the day you release the weight of comparison and start celebrating who you are. You are not behind. You are not less than. You are right where God wants you—becoming everything He created you to be.

Action

- **Unfollow Comparison:** Take a break from any media or environment that stirs up self-doubt.
- **Disconnect Approval from Comparison:** The next time you catch yourself comparing, ask: *Am I admiring them, or am I auditioning for approval I already have from God?* Write down the difference.
- **Affirm Yourself:** Write down 3 things that make you uniquely you—and thank God for them.
- **Celebrate Others:** Bless someone you've compared yourself to—pray for them or send an encouraging message.
- **Speak Life:** Each morning for the next week, speak

this truth: *"God, thank You for making me exactly who I am."*

Declaration

I break the chains of comparison today. I will no longer measure my worth against others. I am fearfully made, purposefully placed, and fully equipped for the life God has called me to live. My value was never determined by how I performed next to someone else. I retire the scoreboard today. I will walk in confidence, celebrate others without shrinking, and honor my own journey with joy. I am enough—because He is more than enough in me.

Journal Prompt

Where have I been comparing myself to others? Has your need for approval turned comparison into a constant measuring stick? What truth does God want you to embrace about your unique identity—apart from anyone else's highlight reel?

____

____

____

____

____

11

The Fear of Being Too Much

Somewhere along the way, I started believing a dangerous lie: That who I was—fully, emotionally, unapologetically—was too much.

Too sensitive. Too emotional. Too needy. Too deep. Too intense.

So I began to shrink—not in body, but in presence. I softened my voice, clipped my desires down to bite-sized pieces, and rehearsed neutral expressions in the mirror so no one would mistake my emotion for chaos. In conversations, I diluted myself the way you stir water into juice: enough color to seem real, but never enough to overwhelm.

I apologized for tearing up. I apologized for asking for clarity. I apologized for wanting connection.

Because somewhere inside, I believed that fullness made me a burden. And sometimes, the world confirmed it.

I noticed the way people shifted in their seats when I spoke from the heart. The way eyes darted toward the floor when emotion thickened the air. I watched conversations skim across the surface like stones skipping over water—never sinking, never honest—and I learned to follow their lead. Vulnerability, I discovered, was something many people admired from afar but backed away from up close.

So I tucked my deeper self into the quiet.

Not gone—just contained.

The passionate parts. The questioning parts. The aching, fiery, too-honest-for-safety parts. I kept them sealed behind practiced smiles and well-timed "I'm fine"s. I held my breath when I wanted to break open. I swallowed words meant to be spoken out loud.

But hiding came at a cost.

The more I edited myself, the more disconnected I became—from my own body, my voice, my truth. I felt unseen because I wasn't showing up. I felt unloved because the version of me people accepted wasn't even real. Loneliness grew not from a lack of people, but from the absence of myself.

One night, after a long day of pretending I was okay, I found myself standing at my kitchen sink, rinsing a coffee mug I never actually drank from. The house was quiet except for the low hum of the refrigerator. My hands were trembling—not from fear, but from the weight of everything I'd held in.

Then something simple, almost insignificant happened:

A single tear dropped into the soapy water.

And instead of wiping it away, instead of swallowing hard and gathering myself like I always did, **I let my body move**—fully, honestly—for the first time in years. My shoulders sagged. My breath shuddered. I gripped the counter and finally allowed myself to feel the truth I kept burying:

I was tired of being a watered-down version of myself.

That tear snapping against the stainless steel sink was the sound of something breaking open.

The moment I realized that hiding was hurting me more than honesty ever could.

What I Know Now

I was never "too much." I was simply **too alive** for people who preferred life muted. Too expressive for those who were numb. Too deep for those terrified of their own internal oceans.

But that does not make me wrong. It makes me whole.

I am layered. Emotional and strong. Tender and fierce. I feel deeply because I care deeply. I love with intensity because I remember what it felt like to go without it. I speak truth because silence almost swallowed me.

And anyone who calls that "too much" is simply not meant to hold all that I am.

Healing now looks like reclaiming the space I once surrendered.

It looks like telling the truth the first time.
Letting tears fall without apology.
Taking up emotional room without shrinking into the corners.

I don't need to dim to be loved.
I don't need to compress myself to be accepted.
I don't need to apologize for existing in full volume.

Selah Moment: Surrendering Control

Scripture

Therefore do not worry about tomorrow, for tomorrow will worry about itself. Each day has enough trouble of its own. — Matthew 6:34 NIV

Reflection

Worry is often our attempt to secure what feels uncertain. We cling to control because we fear what might happen if we don't. We play out scenarios in our mind, trying to anticipate every outcome, every disappointment, every possibility. But the truth is—much of what we fear never even comes to pass, and the energy we spend trying to manage the unknown only drains us of strength for today.

I used to believe that if I didn't hold everything together, everything would fall apart. I worried about decisions, relationships, finances, the future, and even things I had no power to change. I lived in a constant state of tension—gripping life with both hands, exhausted from playing the role of God without even realizing it.

And for those of us who were told we were "too much," control becomes the way we manage how people experience us. We edit, we filter, we shrink—all to control the outcome of being accepted. But that's just another form of worry—the fear that if we let go and show up fully, we'll be rejected for it.

But something shifted when I started trusting God with what I couldn't see. Peace didn't come because everything became predictable; it came because I learned to rest in the One who already knows tomorrow. God isn't asking us to pretend life isn't hard—He's asking us to trust that He is present in every moment, fully aware of what we need, and perfectly capable of carrying what we cannot.

Letting go is not giving up. It's choosing to believe that God is who He says He is—faithful, intentional, and already in your tomorrow. When you release your grip, you make room for His peace. And when you stop trying to control everything, you finally experience the freedom of being held by a God who never loses control.

Action

- **Name your worry.** Write down the specific thing you've been trying to control—be honest and specific.

- **Release the Need to Manage How People See You:** Write down one area where you've been controlling your image — dimming your emotions, editing your words, shrinking your presence.

Surrender it to God and ask Him to give you the courage to show up unfiltered.

- **Pray over it daily for the next week.** Each time anxiety rises, surrender it back to God in prayer.
- **Practice presence.** Choose one moment today to slow down—breathe, pause, and remind yourself: *"God is here with me right now."*
- **Release the "what ifs."** When your mind jumps ahead, gently bring your thoughts back to today with a grounding scripture (Matthew 6:34, Psalm 46:10, or Phillppians 4:6-7).
- **Take one small step of trust.** Do something today that shows you are releasing control—rest, delegate, pause, or simply choose not to rush ahead in fear.

Declaration

I release the weight of tomorrow into God's hands. I lay down fear, worry, and the urge to control. God is already in my future, and He is faithful. I choose peace over panic and trust over anxiety. I release the need to control how others experience me. I was never too much—I was trying to manage what was never mine to carry. I surrender the performance and trust God with how I'm received. Today,

I rest knowing that God is carrying what I was never meant to hold.

Journal

What am I trying to control right now, and why does it feel hard to release? Have you been controlling how much of yourself you show the world? How does that need for control show up in your daily life—physically, mentally, or emotionally?

Selah Moment: Finding Peace in God's Presence

Scripture

Do not be anxious about anything, but in every situation, by prayer and petition, with thanksgiving, present your requests to God. And the peace of God, which transcends all understanding, will guard your hearts and your minds in Christ Jesus. — Philippians 4:6–7 NIV

Reflection

Anxiety whispers lies that make us feel alone, overwhelmed, and out of control. It convinces us that we have to solve everything, fix everything, and carry everything on our own. But God invites us into a different way—a way of release instead of striving, surrender instead of spiraling, peace instead of pressure.

Peace doesn't come because every situation is perfect. Peace doesn't show up when life becomes painless or predictable. Peace comes from God's presence—steady, strong, and unchanging. When we bring our worries to Him through honest prayer, we're not just venting our fears; we're transferring the weight of them into hands far more capable than ours.

I've had nights when anxiety held my mind hostage—when my heart pounded, my thoughts raced, and rest felt impossible. But I learned that peace isn't something I have to chase; it's something God gives when I choose to bring my whole heart to Him. The moment I opened my hands and poured out my fears, His peace met me—quietly but powerfully. It didn't always make sense, and it didn't always remove the situation, but it guarded my heart like a shield.

God's peace doesn't just settle your mind; it strengthens your spirit. It doesn't just soothe your thoughts; it stabilizes your soul. He promises a peace so deep and steady that it surpasses understanding—meaning it may not always align with what you see, but it will anchor you in what is true. When anxiety demands your attention, let it become a reminder to go to the One who holds your heart.

Action

- **Create a quiet moment today.** Turn off distractions, breathe deeply, and intentionally invite God into your anxiety.
- **Write down your specific worries.** Name them clearly—there is power in bringing them into the light.
- **Pray through each worry one by one.** Present

them to God honestly, asking Him to carry what you cannot.

- **Add thanksgiving.** Acknowledge God's past faithfulness—this shifts your focus from fear to trust.
- **Practice release.** Visualize placing each worry in God's hands and letting Him take the weight of it.
- **Return to this moment whenever anxiety rises.** Let prayer be your first response, not your last resort.

Declaration

I choose prayer over panic and surrender over fear. God's peace surrounds and strengthens me. I release every anxious thought and invite His presence into my mind and my heart. My worries do not control me—God does. Today, I walk in a peace that is deeper than understanding and stronger than anything that comes against me.

Journal

What worries or fears have been weighing on you lately? When does anxiety hit you the hardest—morning, night, or during certain situations?

12

When Silence Becomes a Language

Silence started as protection. When I was young, it felt safer than speaking. Safer than asking. Safer than risking the sting of being dismissed…or worse, not heard at all. Words were unpredictable. But silence—silence was something I could control.

So I held my tongue. I tucked away the things that hurt. I learned to want less, need less, show less.

In a house full of noise—slurred words leaking through thin walls, cabinets slamming, tension humming like an electrical current—you'd think silence wouldn't stand a chance. But I found mine in the small spaces. I learned to disappear without ever leaving the room. Like the night I sat on the edge of my bed, listening to voices rise and furniture shift, holding my breath as if the smallest sound from me would make things worse. That was the moment I learned stillness kept me safe

What Silence Looked Like in Everyday Life

Silence became my language long before I ever understood I was speaking it. It looked like:

- Nodding instead of answering when someone asked if I was okay.
- Laughing off comments that cut deeper than I let on.
- Tiptoeing through the kitchen, steadying my breathing so no one heard emotion in it.
- Cleaning up messes I didn't make so no one had a reason to raise their voice.
- Sitting at the dinner table with questions in my throat but only passing the salt.
- Practicing calmness in the mirror, rehearsing stillness the way others rehearsed lines in a play.

My silence said everything I was too scared to speak. I talked through lowered eyes, pressed lips, careful movements—the way I hugged the edges of a room like an object placed on a shelf. My silence wasn't just the absence of sound; it was a posture. A strategy. A way of managing the world so it didn't swallow me whole.

And for a while, it worked. It kept the peace. It steadied the ground. It helped me survive.

But silence isn't neutral. It says: "I don't trust my voice." "I don't want to be a burden." "I'm used to being invisible." "My feelings don't matter."

And the longer I spoke that language, the more fluent I became in disappearing. I didn't just quiet the pain—I muted the joy, the desire, the truth. I muted **myself.** I believed silence made me strong, but it only kept me small.

The Moment Everything Shifted

The first time I told my story, it was barely more than a whisper. My hands wouldn't stop trembling. My throat tightened around words that had lived in the dark for years.

I remember sitting across from someone who asked a simple question— "Can you tell me what really happened?"

For a moment, the old language surged back: *Stay quiet. Stay safe. Stay small.*

But something in me knew that staying silent was costing me more than speaking ever could. So, I let the words come. At first, one sentence. Then another. And suddenly, the dam I had built my whole life began to crack.

My voice shook, but it didn't break. My heart raced, but I didn't run. The world didn't explode. No one turned away.

In that fragile moment—my truth trembling in the air between us—something holy unfolded. I was met not with judgment, but compassion. Not with rejection, but understanding. Not with emptiness, but connection.

For the first time, I felt what it was like to be seen without having to shrink. Every time I speak my truth now, I reclaim a piece of the girl who learned to disappear.

Learning a New Language

I am learning the language of honesty, of emotion, of presence. The language of self-worth.

But silence still tries to slip back in—especially in moments when I feel unsteady, when someone's tone changes, when conflict arises and the old instinct whispers, *Just make yourself small again.*

But now, I recognize that voice for what it is: a ghost from a life I no longer live.

I pause. I breathe. And I gently remind myself:

Your voice matters. Your story matters. You matter.

Selah Moment: Learning to Speak After Years of Silence

Scripture

He lifted me out of the slimy pit, out of the mud and mire; He set my feet on a rock and gave me a firm place to stand. He put a new song in my mouth, a hymn of praise to our God. Many will see and fear the Lord and put their trust in him.— Psalm 40:2-3 NIV

Reflection

For years, silence was the safest language I knew. I spoke it fluently—through lowered eyes, pressed lips, careful movements, and rehearsed calmness. I believed that staying quiet kept the peace, kept me safe, kept me from being too much. But the longer I stayed silent, the more I disappeared—not just from others, but from myself.

Silence doesn't just mute pain. It mutes joy, desire, truth, and purpose. And what starts as protection slowly becomes a prison. God didn't create you to live muted. He gave you a voice—not by accident, but with intention. And every word you've been holding back has weight, meaning, and power.

Speaking after years of silence isn't easy. Your throat tightens. Your hands shake. The old instinct screams: *Stay quiet. Stay small. Stay safe.* But there comes a moment when staying silent costs more than speaking ever could. And that's when healing begins—not when the fear disappears, but when your voice moves through it anyway.

You were created with intention, on purpose, for a purpose. Nothing about your story or your voice is a mistake. The world needs what you've been holding in. And God is awakening your voice—morning by morning—to speak life where silence once lived.

Action

- **Name the Silence:** Write down one thing you've been holding in — something you've never said out loud. You don't have to share it with anyone yet. Just let it exist outside of you.

- **Speak Life:** Say one honest thing today that you would normally swallow. It can be small — a feeling, a need, a boundary. Let your voice practice being free.

- **Identify the Old Language:** Write down the ways silence still shows up in your life—nodding when you disagree, laughing off what hurts, shrinking in conflict. Recognize the pattern so you can interrupt it.

- **Journal Gratitude for Your Voice:** Write down three moments where speaking up changed something for the better—even if your voice shook.
- **Create a Truth Card:** Write this down and place it somewhere visible: *"My voice matters. My silence is over."*

Declaration

I am no longer fluent in disappearing. The silence that once protected me no longer defines me. God has given me a voice—not to stay hidden, but to speak truth, to heal, and to be heard. I release the old language of fear, smallness, and invisibility. I am learning to speak, and every word I say out loud takes back something that silence stole. My story matters. My truth matters. My voice matters. And I will use it — shaking, trembling, and all.

Journal

Where has silence been running your life? What have you been holding in that needs to come out? What would it feel like to let your voice take up space—not perfectly, but honestly?

Selah Moment: Walking in the Power of the Holy Spirit

Scripture

But you will receive power when the Holy Spirit comes on you; and you will be my witnesses in Jerusalem, and in all Judea and Samaria, and to the ends of the earth. — Acts 1:8 NIV

Reflection

The Holy Spirit is not a distant force or a gentle suggestion—He is the very power of God living within you. Jesus didn't leave us to navigate life on our own; He sent the Holy Spirit so we could live with courage, strength, clarity, and supernatural boldness. The same Spirit that empowered the early church, performed miracles, and raised Jesus from the dead is the Spirit who dwells in *you.*

Before the Holy Spirit transformed my heart, I often felt weak—unsure of myself, uncertain of my calling, and afraid to speak or step out. I believed in God, but I didn't yet understand the power available to me through Him. When fear rose, I shrank back. When doubts came, I felt paralyzed. I thought my life had to be lived out of my own effort, my own strength, my own voice.

But everything changed when I learned to rely on the Holy Spirit. He gives courage where fear once lived. He gives direction when confusion sets in. He gives boldness when insecurity tries to silence you. He comforts, convicts, teaches, strengthens, and empowers you to live out the calling God has placed on your life.

You are not powerless.

You are not empty.

You are not alone.

The Spirit of God Himself lives in you—not to make you perfect, but to make you *powerful*. When you lean into Him, you step into your identity. When you ask for His leading, He gives you wisdom no human could offer. When you open your heart to His presence, He fills you with confidence that does not come from you, but flows through you.

The Holy Spirit is not just for "spiritual moments"—He empowers your everyday life. He emboldens your decisions, your conversations, your healing, your purpose, and your witness. You carry divine power everywhere you go. And when you remember that, everything changes.

Action

- **Invite the Holy Spirit into your day.** Start your morning with: *"Holy Spirit, fill me, lead me, and empower me today."*

- **Listen for His prompts.** Pay attention to nudges—encourage someone, speak truth, forgive, pause, or act in boldness.

- **Ask for specific strength.** What area feels weak? Pray: *"Holy Spirit, empower me in this place."*

- **Declare Scripture over yourself.** Verses like Acts 1:8, Romans 8:11, and 2 Timothy 1:7 remind you of the power within you.

- **Step out in faith.** Do one thing today that requires courage—even a small step—trusting the Spirit to guide you.

- **Reflect on His presence.** At the end of the day, write how you saw the Holy Spirit move, guide, or strengthen you.

Declaration

I am filled with the power of the Holy Spirit. God's strength flows through me, His wisdom guides me, and His boldness rises within me. Fear does not limit me, insecurity does not silence me, and doubt does not hold me back. I walk with confidence—not by my own ability, but through the power of God alive in me. Today, I step boldly into my calling, empowered, equipped, and led by the Holy Spirit.

Journal

Where in my life do I feel weak or powerless—and how might the Holy Spirit want to empower me there? When have I felt the Holy Spirit nudging, guiding, or strengthening me?

13

Becoming the Mother I Needed

I didn't grow up with the kind of mother I needed. I grew up with a woman who was hurting, drowning, numbing herself with a bottle because it was the only way she knew how to cope. She was broken, and her brokenness left cracks in me. I remember one night standing in the doorway, holding up a picture I had drawn for her, hoping she'd look up and smile—but her eyes were glassy, fixed on the television, the bottle resting against her knee. I lowered the picture, realizing even then that the mother I needed wasn't coming.

So, when I became a mother, I carried both a longing and a fear. The longing to give my child what I never had: love that stays. And the fear that I would repeat the same cycles. That I wasn't enough. That my wounds would bleed into her world the way my mother did into mine. But the moment I held her in my arms, something shifted—an undeniable clarity that the cycle could end with me, that love could heal what history tried to repeat, and that I had the power to choose a different way forward.

I wasn't a perfect mother. I made mistakes—some I still grieve. There were moments when I reacted out of my pain instead of from peace. Times I was distracted, overwhelmed, unsure. I did the best I could with what I had, but there are days I still ask myself, *Was it enough? Did I love her well? Did I protect her the way I needed someone to protect me?*

But here's what I know for sure: *My daughter is my world.* She is the light that pulled me forward when I could have stayed stuck. She is the reason I began to heal—to grow, to fight for a different future. She is the one who taught me what love looks like when it's raw and real and unconditional.

I may not have had the blueprint for how to be a healthy mother. But I had the heart. I had the will. I had the desire to love her deeply, fiercely, and in every way, I didn't feel loved myself. And that love changed me.

It made me brave enough to look at my past and say, *it stops with me.* It made me soften where life had hardened me. It made me strong in the ways I once believed I couldn't be.

I wanted to be the mother I never had. And though I didn't get it perfect, I showed up. I stayed. I loved her with everything I had.

Being her mother is a privilege I don't take lightly. She may never know all the things I fought through to give her better. But I hope she always knows this: **She is loved. She**

is safe. And she is worth every ounce of healing I've fought for.

In loving her, I became the mother I once cried for. And in choosing to heal—piece by piece, day by day—I'm giving her the version of me I never had growing up: whole, present, steady. Not the scraps I fought to survive on, but the best of me...the part I never knew I was allowed to become.

Selah Moment: Breaking Free from Perfectionism

Scripture

Come to me, all you who are weary and burdened, and I will give you rest. Take my yoke upon you and learn from me, for I am gentle and humble in heart, and you will find rest for your souls.
— Matthew 11:28–29 NIV

Reflection

Perfectionism is a quiet thief. It steals joy, peace, confidence, and even the ability to receive love. It convinces you that you must perform to be accepted, achieve to be valued, and hold everything together to be worthy. It whispers, *"Do more. Be more. Try harder."* And the weight of that expectation becomes exhausting.

Jesus never asked us to be perfect. He asked us to come. He invites the weary—not the polished. He invites the burdened—not the flawless. He invites the overwhelmed—not the put-together.

I spent years trying to outrun my imperfections—trying to fix myself, earn approval, and reach some imaginary standard that always moved just out of reach. I measured my worth by my performance and constantly felt "not enough." The pressure was relentless, and it left me drained—physically, emotionally, and spiritually. Especially in motherhood. When you didn't have a blueprint for what a healthy mother looks like, perfectionism becomes the overcorrection — the desperate need to get it right because getting it wrong feels like repeating the cycle you swore to break.

But Jesus offers a different path. He offers rest—not the surface-level kind, but soul-deep rest that steadies your heart and quiets the noise in your mind. His "yoke," meaning His way of living, is gentle, light, and rooted in grace. It allows you to breathe again. It frees you from the fear of failure. It reminds you that your worth isn't earned—it's given.

Rest doesn't come from doing everything right. Rest comes from being held by the One who is already enough.

Jesus isn't asking you to prove yourself. He's asking you to trust Him with the places where you feel inadequate. He wants to teach you how to live from grace instead of striving, from surrender instead of pressure, from love instead of fear. When you release perfectionism and cling to Him, your soul finds the rest you've been longing for.

Action

- **Identify one area of your life** where perfectionism is draining you. (Motherhood, work, appearance, relationships, faith, etc.)

- **Write down the unrealistic expectation you've been placing on yourself.**
- **Ask Jesus to help you release it.** Pray: *"Lord, teach me Your gentle way. Help me choose rest over pressure."*
- **Replace perfection with progress.** Choose one small, doable action today that reflects grace instead of striving.
- **Practice deep rest.** Create a moment of stillness today—sit quietly, breathe deeply, or meditate on Matthew 11:28–29.
- **Celebrate imperfection.** Notice something you did imperfectly today and thank God for loving you right there.

Declaration

I release the weight of perfectionism and surrender my striving to Jesus. I am loved in my weakness and valued beyond my performance. I did not have to be a perfect mother to be a good one. Showing up, staying, and choosing to love differently than I was loved — that was enough. God's grace covers me, carries me, and strengthens me. I choose rest instead of pressure, peace instead of perfection, and I walk in the gentle rhythm of Jesus—secure, loved, and free.

Journal

Where in my life do I feel the most pressure to be perfect? Has the fear of repeating your past made perfectionism feel like the only option—especially in how you love and parent? How does that pressure affect your peace?

____

____

____

____

____

____

____

____

____

____

____

____

____

____

____

____

Selah Moment: Embracing God's Timing

Scripture

There is a time for everything, and a season for every activity under the heavens… — Ecclesiastes 3:1 NIV

Reflection

Waiting is one of the hardest parts of our walk with God. We love clarity, progress, and immediate answers. But God often works in seasons—slowly, intentionally, and beautifully. His timing rarely matches ours, yet it is always, without fail, perfect.

We struggle not because God is late, but because we don't see what He sees. We feel the tension of "not yet" and assume something is wrong—wrong with us, wrong with the situation, wrong with our faith. But God is the God of process, and He cares more about who you're becoming than how quickly you arrive.

Every season has purpose.

The waiting seasons teach trust.
The stretching seasons build endurance.
The quiet seasons deepen faith.
The painful seasons produce growth.
And the joyful seasons remind us of God's goodness.

I've had moments where I begged God for movement, for answers, for change—wondering if He had forgotten me. I questioned His silence, confused by delays that didn't make sense. But looking back, every season of waiting prepared me for what was coming. Not one moment was wasted. The delay was protection. The pause was preparation. And sometimes God's timing includes the years it takes to become the person your family needs you to be. The healing didn't come overnight—but every step of it was preparing me to love my daughter the way I always wanted to be loved. The slow place was the safe place. His timing has never failed me—not once.

God is not withholding from you; He is aligning things for you.
He is not late; He is precise.
He is not ignoring your prayers; He is working in ways you cannot see.
If you could see the whole picture, you would thank Him for every "not yet."

The same God who hung the stars, orchestrates creation, and orders the seasons is ordering the timing of your life. You can rest in that. You can breathe in that. You can trust Him in that.

Action

- **Identify the area where waiting feels hardest**

right now. Be honest—name the emotion that comes with it (fear, frustration, impatience, doubt).

- **Pray specifically over that area.** Ask God to align your heart with His timing and give you peace in the process.
- **Look back and remember.** Write down a past moment when God came through at the perfect time—it will strengthen your faith right now.
- **Release the need for control.** Say aloud: *"God, I surrender the timeline. Have Your way."*
- **Embrace your current season.** Ask God what He wants to teach you right now instead of focusing on what you're waiting for.
- **Practice patience today.** Choose one small action—pause before reacting, slow down a rushed moment, or silence a "what if" thought.

Declaration

I trust the God who holds my seasons. His timing is perfect, His plans are good, and His faithfulness never fails. I release my timelines, expectations, and need for control. God is working in ways I cannot see, and He will open every door at the appointed time. I trust that every season of my healing—even the painful ones—was shaping me into the parent, the person, and the purpose God always intended. I walk in peace, patience, and confidence—knowing He is never late, always intentional, and forever faithful.

Journal

What area of my life am I struggling to trust God's timing in? Can you see how God used your healing journey to prepare you for the role you carry now? What emotions rise up when things feel delayed?

____

____

____

____

____

____

____

____

____

____

____

____

____

____

14

Breaking Generational Curses

Some things run in families besides eye color and last names. Pain. Addiction. Silence. Shame. Emotional absence. They're passed down like heirlooms—unspoken, but deeply felt.

A generational curse isn't just a pattern—it's a spiritual and emotional cycle that repeats through families. Scripture talks about how sin, trauma, and broken patterns can travel through generations until someone interrupts it. Exodus 34:7 describes iniquity being "visited upon the children and the children's children," not as punishment, but as the consequence of unhealed patterns that flow downward until someone stops them.

My mother didn't wake up one day and choose to be broken. She was shaped by her own story, her own wounds, her own survival.

But when those wounds go unhealed, they don't disappear—they get passed down. Sometimes in words. Sometimes in silence. Always in weight.

If you've ever wondered where the heaviness in your own family began, start by paying attention to the patterns—the things that repeat themselves without anyone ever deciding they would. Notice the moments where you swallow your voice the same way someone before you did. Notice the fears you carry that don't feel like they started with you. Look at the behaviors that feel inherited: the anger that erupts too quickly, the love that comes with conditions, the silence that settles where truth should live. Generational curses aren't always dramatic—they're often subtle, woven into the rhythms of everyday life. When you trace those threads back, you begin to see which pieces belong to you… and which ones were handed to you without your consent. That awareness is the first crack in the cycle, the first doorway to choosing differently.

I grew up under the shadow of those patterns. And for a while, I lived like I had no other choice—like this was just the way it would always be. Trauma became normal. Dysfunction became familiar. Love and fear lived in the same house. And I thought that surviving was the best I could hope for.

But one day, something shifted. Maybe it was the ache of watching my daughter grow up and knowing I didn't want her to carry what I carried. Maybe it was the whisper in my soul that said, *there has to be more.* Maybe it was God. Or maybe it was all of the above. What I know is this: **I made a decision.**

The pain stops here. The silence ends with me. The curse breaks now.

I decided to do the hard work—to feel what I had buried, to grieve what I never got, to forgive without forgetting, to heal even though it hurt. I chose therapy. Prayer. Boundaries. Tears. Truth. I chose to parent differently, to speak life instead of fear, to ask for help, to show up—imperfect but committed. Healing required simple, everyday courage: like actually pulling my daughter into my arms and holding her when she melted down, choosing closeness instead of shutting down; and looking into the mirror on the days I felt unworthy and speaking out loud, "I am loved. I am chosen. I am enough." And when I didn't know what to do, I leaned on the reminder in Psalm 34:18—that the Lord is close to the brokenhearted—and let that truth guide me toward becoming the mother my child needed

Breaking generational curses doesn't mean pretending the past didn't happen. It means refusing to let it control the future. It means choosing healing even when you never saw it modeled. It means raising your children with gentleness when you were raised in chaos. It means telling the truth, even when your family made silence the rule. It means becoming who you needed—so your children don't have to recover from you.

It's not easy. Some days, it feels like walking uphill with a weight no one else can see. But every choice I make to love, to grow, to be present—that's me swinging the hammer at the chain. That's me breaking it.

And every time I speak, write, cry, pray, or forgive… I'm creating a new legacy.

You cannot break what you won't name. you cannot heal what you won't face. And you cannot change a legacy you're still pretending didn't wound you.

Selah Moment: Choosing to Break the Cycle

Scripture

Therefore, if anyone is in Christ, the new creation has come: The old has gone, the new is here! — 2 Corinthians 5:17 NIV

Reflection

Some things are passed down without permission—pain, silence, addiction, emotional absence, fear. They move through families like invisible currents, shaping how we love, how we cope, and how we see ourselves. And for a long time, you may have believed that the cycle was your destiny—that because it happened to you, it would happen through you.

But God is in the business of making all things new. The moment you became aware of the pattern was the moment the cycle lost its power over your future. Awareness is the first crack. And every choice you make after that—to heal, to speak, to parent differently, to love differently, to show up even when it's hard—is another swing at the chain.

Breaking a cycle doesn't mean you won't feel the pull of what's familiar. It means you choose differently anyway. It means you grieve what you never received while building something new for those coming after you. It means you stop waiting for someone else to fix what was broken and you become the one who says: it ends here.

This is holy work. It's exhausting, uncomfortable, and sometimes lonely. But every time you choose therapy over silence, boundaries over dysfunction, truth over pretending, and presence over numbing—you are writing a new legacy. And the generations after you will breathe easier because you had the courage to break what was never yours to carry.

Action

- **Name the Cycle:** Write down one generational pattern you've identified in your family—addiction, silence, emotional absence, fear, anger, conditional love. Name it clearly so it loses its power in the dark.

- **Trace It Back:** Without blame, reflect on where the pattern started. Who carried it before you? Understanding the origin brings compassion—for them and for yourself.

- **Declare the Break:** Write a statement of freedom: *"This cycle ends with me. I choose a different path for my life and for the generations after me."* Speak it out loud.

- **Take One Healing Step:** Whether it's therapy, prayer, a hard conversation, setting a boundary, or forgiving someone—do one thing today that moves you away from the old pattern and toward the new.

- **Celebrate the Progress:** Write down one way you've already broken the cycle—even if it feels small. You are further than you think.

Declaration

I am a cycle breaker. The pain that was passed down to me does not get to pass through me. I choose healing over hiding, truth over silence, gratitude over comparison, and acceptance over rejection. I choose thanksgiving over jealousy, freedom over addiction, and courage over complacency. In Christ, I am a new creation — the old has gone and the new is here. My heart is full because God is faithful, generous, and always working. God has been good to me, He is good to me, and He will continue to be. The chain breaks with me, and everything after me will be different because I had the courage to choose differently. Today, I walk in contentment, peace, and joy — with a grateful heart that sees God's hand in every season.

Journal

What generational pattern have you been carrying that didn't start with you? What would it look like to officially break that cycle — not perfectly, but intentionally? What new legacy do you want to build for those who come after you?

Selah Moment: Finding Joy in the Journey

Scripture

Do not grieve, for the joy of the Lord is your strength. — Nehemiah 8:10 NIV

Reflection

Joy is not the absence of hardship—joy is the presence of God in the midst of it. Life brings moments that shake us, break us, and stretch us in ways we never expected. Grief, disappointment, delays, and unknowns can make joy feel distant or even impossible. But God doesn't ask us to deny our pain; He invites us to anchor ourselves in a joy that is deeper than circumstances.

The joy of the Lord is not a feeling you have to force—it is a strength He gives. It's the assurance that God is still good, still near, still working, and still faithful even when life feels heavy. Joy is the quiet confidence that God is in control when we aren't. It's the supernatural ability to stand in peace, hope, and gratitude when everything around you says you should fall apart.

There was a long season when joy felt unreachable to me. I smiled on the outside but struggled inside. I didn't understand how people could talk about joy when I felt exhausted, hurt, or confused. But slowly, God showed me that joy wasn't something I had to create—it was something I could receive. Joy began to rise in the silence, in the surrender, in the gratitude for small things, in the whispers of His presence reminding me, "I am here."

And when you're doing the hard work of breaking generational cycles—facing what was passed down to you, choosing to heal, choosing to parent differently, choosing to live differently—joy is what keeps you going. Not because the work is easy, but because every chain you break is proof that God is doing something new in you.

Even in waiting, joy can bloom. Even in heartache, joy can steady you. Even in the unknown, joy can strengthen you.

This kind of joy doesn't ignore reality—it transforms it. It shifts your focus from what's wrong to Who is with you. It becomes the strength that holds you together when you feel like you're unraveling. The joy of the Lord is not fragile—it is fierce. It is a gift. And it is yours.

Action

- **Practice gratitude intentionally.** Write down one to three things you're thankful for today—large or small.

- **Pause for presence.** Take a quiet moment and

invite God into your emotions, especially if they feel heavy.

- **Shift your focus.** When a negative thought rises, counter it with one truth about God's character His goodness, faithfulness, or nearness.
- **Find joy in the breaking.** Write down one cycle you've broken or one step of healing you've taken—and celebrate it. That's not just progress. That's joy.
- **Look for joy in the ordinary.** A warm drink, a kind word, a moment of laughter, a sunset—notice and receive them as gifts.
- **Share joy.** Speak encouragement to someone, smile at someone, or send a thoughtful message—joy grows when we give it away.
- **Declare truth when your feelings disagree.** Speak Scripture aloud to remind your heart that joy is rooted in God, not in circumstance.

Declaration

I choose joy—not because life is perfect, but because God is present. His joy strengthens me, sustains me, and lifts me above every heaviness. I refuse to let fear, grief, or discouragement steal what God has given. Every chain I break, every cycle I end, every step I take toward healing is a reason to rejoice. Today, I walk in confidence, gratitude, and peace—anchored in the joy of the Lord, which is my unshakable strength and my song.

Journal

What has been trying to steal my joy recently? Can you find joy in the hard work of breaking cycles—even when it's exhausting? How has God shown you His presence even in difficult seasons?

___

___

___

___

___

___

___

___

___

___

___

___

___

15

This Is Where It Ends—and Begins

I've carried a lot. Pain that wasn't mine. Silence that kept me small. Guilt I never earned. Shame that settled in my bones before I could even spell the word.

I've lived through things that tried to take me out—from the inside. Molestation at seven. A mother lost to addiction. Years of performing, pleasing, and pretending just to feel safe. To feel loved. To feel *enough.*

I didn't always handle it perfectly. I made mistakes. I passed on pain. I survived in ways that didn't always look like healing. I wasn't always the mother I wanted to be—but I never stopped loving. Never stopped trying. Never stopped hoping there could be more.

And there *is* more.

Because healing is not just about what I've walked through. It's about what I've walked out of. Somewhere along the way, God began whispering truth louder than my fear—reminding me that survival is not my identity, and brokenness is not my inheritance.

I am not the little girl who cried in silence anymore. I am not the teenager who blamed herself. I am not the woman who had to beg to be chosen. I am not the reflection distorted by shame or the echo of anyone else's choices.

I am healing. I am whole—even with the cracks. I am learning to let joy settle where fear once lived. I'm speaking up in places I used to shrink. I'm choosing honesty over silence and connection over hiding.

And I am the curse breaker. It didn't stop with my mother. Or her mother. It stops with me.

I've found the strength to say what no one before me could say: *This happened. It hurt. But it didn't end me.* I've found the courage to turn my pain into purpose, my scars into sacred stories.

To the little girl I was: You didn't deserve what happened. To the woman I became: You did your best, and that was enough.

To the daughter I'm raising: You are why I chose healing over hiding.

And to anyone reading this who sees pieces of your own story in mine—please know this: *You are not alone. You are not broken. You are not too far gone.* You are worthy of love, of safety, of freedom, of joy. You don't have to keep carrying what was handed down to you. You don't have to earn your worth—it's already yours. You don't have to live pretending, shrinking, or surviving.

You can heal. You can speak. You can rewrite your story.

This isn't just the end of my pain. It's the beginning of my freedom.

Your beginning may start with one confession, one tear, one boundary, one prayer. Freedom rarely arrives all at once—it often begins quietly, with one honest step toward the truth.

And if I can break the cycle—*so can you.*

Selah Moment: Walking in Courage

Scripture

Have I not commanded you? Be strong and courageous. Do not be afraid; do not be discouraged, for the Lord your God will be with you wherever you go." — Joshua 1:9 NIV

Reflection

Fear doesn't always show up as panic—it often wears the face of hesitation. It disguises itself as procrastination, perfectionism, or the need for more clarity. It whispers that you're not ready, not enough, not safe. And too often, we listen.

I've spent years letting fear have the final word. I stayed silent when I should've spoken up. I tolerated what made me uncomfortable because I didn't want to make waves. I hid parts of myself because I was afraid of judgment or rejection.

But God's command is clear—it's not a suggestion or a gentle nudge. He *commands* us to be strong and courageous. Not because we're fearless, but because **He is with us.** Courage doesn't come from having all the answers; it comes from trusting the One who does.

I've had to do many things afraid—speaking my truth, setting boundaries, showing up in rooms that once made me shrink. And every time I stepped forward, trembling but obedient, God met me there. Writing this book was one of those steps. Saying out loud what happened at seven, what addiction stole, what silence cost me—that took courage I didn't know I had. But every chapter I wrote was another chain that fell. Courage isn't just about what's ahead. Sometimes it's about finally facing what's behind you and declaring: it didn't end me. Fear might still knock, but now I know: it doesn’t get to drive.

Action

- Identify **one area** in your life where fear has been holding you back—starting a conversation, pursuing a dream, or trusting again.

- Write down the **worst-case scenario** you fear—and then write what’s *more likely* to happen if God is with you.

- Ask yourself: *What’s one small step of courage I can take today?*

- Pray: “God, I give You the fear that has kept me stuck. Help me to walk in Your strength and confidence.”

- Choose a courage verse (like Joshua 1:9) and place it somewhere visible this week.

Declaration

I will not let fear write my story. I am strong, not in my own strength, but in the presence of God who walks beside me. I choose courage over comfort, faith over fear, and obedience over excuses. I am no longer the person who hides. I have spoken my truth, broken the silence, and walked out of every chapter that tried to define me. This is where my courage lives—not in perfection, but in freedom. Wherever I go, God is with me—and that is enough.

Journal

Where has fear been holding me back? What is one area God is calling me to be brave in today?

____

____

____

____

____

____

____

____

____

____

Selah Moment: Stepping into Your Calling

Scripture

And we know that in all things God works for the good of those who love him, who have been called according to his purpose. — Romans 8:28 NIV

Reflection

God wastes absolutely nothing—not your pain, not your past, not your failures, and not your waiting seasons. Every piece of your story is woven into something purposeful, intentional, and deeply personal. When Scripture says "in all things," it means exactly that. Nothing is outside of God's ability to redeem, restore, reroute, or use for your growth and His glory.

Sometimes calling feels intimidating because we assume it requires perfection, confidence, or a flawless past. But God calls us from the exact place we stand—messy, healing, learning, growing, still becoming. Your experiences, your struggles, your breakthroughs, and even your scars have uniquely shaped you for what God is calling you to do.

For a long time, I questioned my value. I wondered if my story disqualified me or if my gifts were too small. But God slowly showed me that my voice carries power because of what I've lived through—not in spite of it. My pain gave me compassion. My healing gave me wisdom. My story gave me strength. And the very parts of my life I wanted to hide became the very things God uses to help others. This book is proof of that. Every wound, every silence, every cycle I broke—it all led here. My calling wasn't waiting for me on the other side of perfection. It was waiting for me on the other side of honesty.

Stepping into your calling isn't about being fearless—it's about being willing. It's choosing to trust that God is working in all things, even when you can't see how. It's taking one step at a time, believing that if God called you to it, He will lead you through it. He doesn't ask you to understand the whole path. He just asks you to take the next faithful step.

When you embrace your calling, you partner with God in the work He is already doing. And that's where purpose becomes powerful.

Action

- **Pray for clarity.** Ask God to show you the next step—not the whole plan—just the next one.

- **Write down experiences that shaped you**—your pain, victories, lessons, and passions. Notice patterns that point toward your purpose.

- **List your God-given strengths.** These may include compassion, leadership, creativity, wisdom, or resilience—nothing is too small.

- **Take one step today.** Send the message. Apply for the opportunity. Share the story. Serve someone. Start the idea.

- **Release perfection.** Remind yourself that God equips the called—He doesn't wait for them to be fully ready.

- **Pay attention to open doors.** When God is calling you somewhere, He confirms it through opportunities, peace, and confirmation in your spirit.

Declaration

I boldly step into the purpose God has placed on my life. Nothing in my story is wasted—God is working all things for my good. From the little girl who cried in silence to the woman who wrote it all down—every piece of my journey has purpose. This is not just the end of my pain. It is the beginning of my calling. I am called, equipped, and supported by the One who leads me. Fear does not define me. Doubt does not stop me. With faith in my heart and

God by my side, I walk confidently into my calling—ready, willing, and empowered to fulfill God's purpose for me.

Journal

What parts of my story have shaped me the most—and how might God use them for purpose? Where do I feel God nudging me to take a step of faith?

Acknowledgements

To my daughter, whose love has always been my anchor and my greatest motivation—thank you for being the light that guides me forward. To Chelsea Strawn, thank you for introducing me to Yosi Publishing and for gently helping me see what I couldn't always see in myself. To Yosi Publishing, I am deeply grateful for taking my scattered journals and transforming them into a real, tangible story—your patience, guidance, and belief in me carried me through every step. To Wendy Lee, thank you for always being there for me, offering steady support when I needed it most. To Charline Bucher, thank you for being such a powerful spiritual leader and for speaking life into me. And above all, to God—thank You for planting this seed in my heart and for transforming my pain into purpose.

About the Author

Veronica Mills is a devoted special education teacher, mother, and woman of faith whose life reflects resilience, compassion, and unwavering trust in God. For years, she has poured patience and strength into the lives of her students, walking alongside children with unique needs and discovering in the process that some of life's greatest lessons are found in quiet perseverance. Teaching has shaped her, softened her, and deepened her understanding of what true strength looks like.

Behind her steady presence is a testimony marked by both pain and redemption.

For much of her life, Veronica carried the weight of childhood trauma that shaped how she viewed herself and the world around her. The years that followed brought painful seasons that left wounds she did not yet know how to name. Shame, fear, and unworthiness became silent chains influencing how she lived and what she believed she deserved.

But her story did not end there.

Today, Veronica stands as a woman who has walked through the fire and emerged stronger. At 48, she looks back with gratitude, recognizing how faithfully God carried her through every dark valley. The freedom she once believed was out of reach has become her lived reality—evidence that God redeems even the most broken places.

Scripture became her anchor. God's Word spoke life into shattered spaces, unraveled long-held lies, and replaced them with truth. Through His grace, despair gave way to healing, and silence gave way to courage.

Her greatest inspiration is her daughter—the light that motivated her healing and the reminder that generational cycles can be broken. Veronica chose wholeness not only for herself, but for the legacy she would pass on.

Through this memoir and devotional, Veronica shares the pain, growth, victories, and freedom that shaped her journey. She writes for the woman who feels trapped by her past, burdened by shame, or silenced by fear. Her prayer is that these pages become a safe place—an invitation to lean into God's truth, release what no longer serves you, and embrace healing.

No matter what you have endured, you are worthy of love, peace, and restoration. Her story is a reminder that God meets us in our darkest places and leads us into freedom.

You are held. You are loved. And you are never alone.

Connect with Veronica

- Facebook: Veronica Mills Shelton
- Instagram: veronicashelton_
- TikTok: veronicamillsshel

www.ingramcontent.com/pod-product-compliance
Lightning Source LLC
LaVergne TN
LVHW020711110826
845149LV00012B/2212